MICROWAVE
•LITE•
MENU COOKBOOK

Delicious Complete Meals
Under 450 Calories

By the Editors of MICROWAVE TIMES

CONTEMPORARY
BOOKS, INC.
CHICAGO ▪ NEW YORK

Library of Congress Cataloging-in-Publication Data

Microwave lite menu cookbook.

   1. Low-calorie diet—Recipes.   2. Microwave
cookery.   I. Microwave times.
RM222.2.M487   1986   641.5'635   86-16740
ISBN 0-8092-4970-7 (pbk.)

Published by Contemporary Books, Inc.
180 North Michigan Avenue, Chicago, Illinois 60601
Manufactured in the United States of America
Library of Congress Catalog Card Number: 86-16740
International Standard Book Number: 0-8092-4970-7

Published simultaneously in Canada by Beaverbooks, Ltd.
195 Allstate Parkway, Valleywood Business Park
Markham, Ontario L3R 4T8 Canada

CONTENTS

PREFACE   v

INTRODUCTION   1

1   MICROWAVE COOKING TIPS   5

2   DAY STARTERS   9

3   FAMILY MEALS   29

4   MINI-MEALS   63

5   MEALS FOR ONE OR TWO   91

6   QUICK AND EASY MEALS   121

7   MAKE-AHEAD MEALS   149

8   FREEZER MEALS   175

9   DESSERTS   205

INDEX   229

PREFACE

Welcome to our second book on "lite" microwave cooking. We think the concept of lite eating has a lot of advantages, and it is a joy to bring you this follow-up book to our first, *Microwave Cooking Lite*.

Even though our meal patterns are changing and we are eating fewer sit-down meals with the entire family present, it is still possible to provide nutritious, healthful food with the help of your microwave oven. This book is written with that in mind. There are traditional meals, but also many mini-meal suggestions and healthful snack ideas to help assure balanced nutrition, even with our busy, on-the-go schedules.

Recipes Unlimited, Inc., is located in Burnsville, Minnesota, where we develop and publish a bimonthly newsletter, *The Microwave Times*, for microwave oven owners. Since our beginning in 1974, our goal has been to help oven owners get the most use from their microwave ovens. We accomplish this through publications like *The Microwave Times* and cookbooks such as this one.

Our test kitchen was the center of the development for this book. Many, many hours have gone into the testing to assure that the recipes will work for you and that the Time Guides are realistic. Once the recipes are perfected, they are tested again by another person to be sure that they are understandable and that the same good results can be obtained.

I am indebted to the staff who helped to make this book a reality. The team working on this book included Nancy L. Gunderson and Nancy J. Johnson from our regular staff, and Diane A. Berg and Mary Memelink, who joined us just for this project. Without their ideas, suggestions, and hours of kitchen testing, this book would not have been possible.

Often, I hear of microwave oven owners who have not progressed beyond heating water or warming leftovers. There are so many more things that can be done with the microwave, and we hope this book will help you to discover some of them. Our meals can be nutritious, attractive, and good-tasting. Incorporating the microwave into the preparation can make the whole process easier and quicker. I invite you not only to page through this book, but also to really use the recipes and menus in your quest for good eating with minimal calories and effort.

—*Janet L. Sadlack*

INTRODUCTION

Lite cooking is not just a single food or a meal here and there, but a whole new way of cooking. It need not be lower-quality or less tasty food. In fact, with all of the good ingredients included in this type of cooking, the emphasis is on quality food with minimal calories, fat, and sugar.

"We are what we eat" is often heard or read, but do we take time to realize how true it is? If we want to be in the best possible physical condition, we must pay attention to what we are eating.

Crash diets and food fads may change our weight or shape for a week or two, but they seldom have a positive long-term effect. To accomplish lasting change, we must alter our daily food intake along with our exercise and rest habits.

Often when we think of healthy eating, we assume that good flavor has been sacrificed. This need not be true; often we improve the flavor when we eliminate some of the excess salt, fat, and sugar that overpower the true flavor present. And once we start using less of these ingredients, it is amazing how good foods taste.

In this book, we have not totally eliminated some of the less nutritious ingredients such as sugar, salt, fat, etc., but used only the quantities necessary to enhance the natural flavor of the food to be prepared. There are lower-calorie versions of many of these ingredients, and they can often be substituted if your diet is more restricted.

Healthy eating means monitoring our entire food consumption. Whether we eat three regular meals or four to five smaller meals each day, it is important to have a balance of protein, vegetables, fruit, grains, and milk products. When limiting calories, it is even more important to be sure that a balance of these food types is included each day.

Exercise is also a key to our well-being, but it does not replace the need to eat well. We gain weight when we consume more calories than our bodies use. Calorie intake and physical activity need to be coordinated to maintain the best possible physical condition. As we age, our caloric needs decrease, which means we need to lower our food intake and/or increase our level of physical activity to prevent having to gradually buy a new wardrobe.

This book is centered around meals to help you achieve a proper balanced diet. Calories are given not only for each recipe, but also for each complete meal. In general, we have planned the meals around the preparation that requires the use of the microwave oven, since these are the recipes and calorie counts included. However, many

1

accompaniments can be added to enhance the meals. Some of the frequently added accompaniments are listed below, along with the approximate number of calories for a serving of each:

Hard roll, 100
½ cup canned fruit, 60
½ cup cooked rice, 100
1 medium baked or boiled potato, 90
½ cup cooked frozen peas, 60
1 carrot, 30
1 apple, 65
1 orange, 60
1 banana, 100
½ cup fruit sherbet, 110
1 slice whole wheat toast, 60
1 glass skim milk, 90
1 glass orange juice, 100
Tossed salad with lite dressing, 40

In planning this book, we have included breakfasts and mini-meals as well as main meal suggestions. Generally, we targeted our calorie ranges as follows:

Breakfast, 200-320 calories
Mini-Meals, 180-320 calories
Main Meals, 190-450 calories
Total, 570-1,090 calories

Your meals need not fall into the same pattern from day to day. For example, you may not have time for a main meal, so you choose to have two mini-meals. Or, instead of a mini-meal or breakfast, you enjoy two main meals. The primary thing is to keep the calorie range within what our bodies require while at the same time eating a balance of the various foods mentioned earlier. The USDA recommends 14 to 26 calories per day for each pound of weight, depending on your activity level. So, if you weigh 120 pounds, your daily calorie needs are probably between 1,700 and 3,000; if you weigh 160 pounds, your calorie needs are in the range of 2,300 to 4,000.

Lite eating is good for us, and family and friends often welcome this type of food. A lite, nutritious meal is often appreciated by guests. Many of the menus included in the "Make-Ahead Meals" and "Family Meals" chapters are ideal for entertaining. Food quality has not been sacrificed—just the extra calories that are not adding flavor or nutritional value to the food. And, if you think the menus are a little skimpy for guests, just prepare extra servings for those with heartier appetites or add other accompaniments to extend the meal.

With our busy schedules, it is often difficult to find time to prepare meals even if we can find time to eat them. The recipes in the "Freezer Meals" chapter will help you keep things on hand so that other family members can heat them even when you are not available to help with the meal preparation. Many are single-serving size, making them ideal for children and adults who might otherwise miss a meal because of school activities, part-time jobs, meetings, and other commitments.

The menus in this book can easily be mixed and matched to best meet your needs. It is most appealing to serve foods that have contrasts in color, flavor, shape, and texture. A meal that is mainly soft and one color is not very appealing. Serve something crunchy and chewy with a soft-textured food and include some white, yellow, and green foods on a plate, and the food will look much more appealing. In the same way, try to incorporate a variety of shapes, with some small chunks and some larger strips.

"We are what we eat," but good planning and tasty recipes are necessary to help assure that the food will be eaten. This book, with its menus, complete step-by-step recipes, and timing suggestions, will help guide you on your way to reaping the benefits from nutritious, lite dining.

CHAPTER
1
MICROWAVE COOKING TIPS

Some of you have probably been using your microwave ovens for years, while others of you are relative newcomers to the appliance. To help answer a few of the questions about microwave cooking techniques and methods used in this book, we encourage you to read through these suggestions and explanations.

TYPES OF OVENS AND POWER LEVELS

The recipes in this book were all tested in 600- to 700-watt countertop microwave ovens. A number of ovens are available today, particularly compact ovens with 400 to 500 watts of cooking power; cooking in these ovens will require slightly more time. A time range is included with the recipes, so start with the shortest time and then add time as needed. The lower-wattage ovens will probably require the maximum time or even a little additional time.

Most of the recipes are cooked on the high- or full-power setting. However, a few foods give better results when a lower-power setting is used. Lower-power settings reduce the microwave energy by pulsing the oven on and off in short intervals so foods cook more slowly. When a high setting also works, we have included these directions in the recipe Tips. Most of these include standing times to slow the cooking or more stirring or rotation.

COOKWARE

We have specified using microwave-safe cookware in our recipes. Many glass and plastic pieces are designed for microwave cooking. For some heating, paper items are very satisfactory. Glass cookware that is not specifically marked for microwave oven use can be checked to see if it is absorbing too much microwave energy. To do this, place the piece in question in the oven along with a cup of water in a separate container. (We use water to represent the food, but don't put it in the container you are checking, as you won't know if the water or the microwaves caused it to become warm.) Then microwave on high for about 45 seconds. Check the warmth of the dish. If it is still fairly cool, it should work well in the microwave. However, if it feels warm, it will absorb too much of the microwave energy, becoming very hot and causing the food to cook too slowly.

ROTATING, STIRRING, AND TURNING

The recipes include reminders for rotating or turning when it may be helpful. This is more important in some ovens than in others and more critical with some foods than with others. Of course, if your oven has a turntable, rotating will not be necessary, but turning and stirring will still be important.

Stirring reminders are more important since they help prevent lumping of sauces and help facilitate even cooking by exchanging the faster-cooking edges with the slower-cooking center.

To make this manipulation easier, on some ovens you can set the time in several intervals with a reminder that will beep when it is time to stir or rotate the food. Otherwise, you may find it helpful just to set the time in shorter intervals so cooking will cease when it is time for the stirring or rotating. Manipulation is seldom a problem as these times give you an opportunity to check the progress of the food as well as to assure an evenly cooked product. If you do forget to stir a sauce, just beat it well to blend out the lumps. When you forget to rotate a cake or casserole, it may just take a few more minutes of cooking time.

RECIPE SIZE

The majority of the recipes in this book were developed for four to five servings. Of course, in the chapter, "Meals for One or Two," the recipes are for smaller quantities. Some of the recipes in the "Freezer Meals" and "Mini-Meals" chapters are geared to individual heating, so the total quantity may be larger or smaller. And, since the "Make-Ahead Meals" chapter has more company-oriented recipes, we increased the number of servings to six to eight.

When you need to serve more or less than the yield of a recipe, just halve or double the ingredients. Find a suitable smaller dish when reducing a recipe; for double recipes it may be necessary to use two dishes. When this is the case, it is best to cook each dish separately. Most timings will increase or decrease proportionately with the change in quantity. A half-recipe usually requires about half plus a little more time. Double recipes require almost double the timing. For example, a one-pound meat loaf that cooks in about eight minutes will probably require four to five minutes when the recipe is halved. Or a two-cup pudding recipe that cooks in about five minutes will take nine to ten minutes when doubled.

SEQUENCE FOR COOKING MEALS

Cooking complete meals in the microwave is more complex than cooking an individual food since normally foods are cooked one at a time, yet we want everything piping hot when served. While at first it might seem quite difficult to achieve, it is actually rather simple once you take advantage of the way the microwave reheats foods. It is no longer necessary to cook everything at the last minute; instead, allow some of the foods to stand and then return them to the microwave for a few minutes to return them to serving temperature.

A few guidelines to keep in mind when preparing several foods for a meal are:

1. Start with the dessert or food that does not need to be served hot.
2. Next microwave the larger, longer-cooking items that reheat well.
3. Then prepare vegetables and other shorter-cooking items that reheat well.
4. Reheat any of the foods prepared earlier that have cooled.
5. Last, heat breads or other items that take very little time and do not reheat well.

The most quickly prepared meals are those in which the microwave is kept in use as much as possible. Thus, it is most efficient to be chopping or mixing for the next step while the food is cooking for a previous step. In the same way, if one food, like a frozen vegetable or baked potato, takes minimal preparation and another, like meat loaf, requires mixing before cooking, it will be faster to cook the vegetable while making the meat loaf. Then reheat the vegetable just before serving.

In the Time Guides, we have suggested a schedule for having all the food hot at the same time. Some menu combinations lend themselves to cooking one food and then another. When there are two foods that require about the same cooking time, it is often helpful to cook one about halfway and then let it stand while cooking the other one. These standing times will help heat the center of foods that are not stirred without overcooking the edges, and usually the split cooking means less total cooking time.

Ovens are available with racks for cooking several foods at once. We have not included directions for this concept for two reasons. First, it usually does not save time when preparing recipes because all of the foods need to be prepared before cooking begins. Second, ovens vary in size and the way the microwaves reach the food, so it is difficult to give directions that will work equally well for all oven brands.

If you have this type of oven, you may want to use it to heat two frozen or make-ahead items. The cooking time will be about double that of a single item, and it will be necessary to reverse the food positions halfway through the cooking since one part of the oven will heat faster than another.

2
DAY STARTERS

Beginning the day with proper nutrition should be utmost in our minds in the morning, but it's hard for many of us to function that early in the day, let alone try to plan and cook a nutritious breakfast. Now, with the help of these recipes, your microwave oven, and on-hand ingredients, you can have quick, lite, satisfying breakfasts geared to getting you and your family going without a lot of hassle.

Our suggested menus fall within the 200- to 320-calorie range. Some are simpler and take less time, for those mornings when time is especially short. Others are perfect for leisurely weekend breakfasts. Entrees can be interchanged with other menus for tasty variety. In several menus, make-ahead steps are suggested to simplify last-minute preparation. Keep in mind that any changes or additions will alter the calorie counts. Most of the recipes use very few dishes; many are cooked and served in the same dish to make cleanup a breeze.

There are several convenience-type breakfast items on the market that microwave well. Some, such as frozen pancakes and waffles, have been incorporated into these menus. Use these frozen products or make your own homemade favorites and freeze to use as needed.

Keep in mind a few tips when preparing typical breakfast foods. Scrambled eggs microwave beautifully. Egg substitutes can be used in many of the recipes if cholesterol is a concern. When cooking eggs, it is helpful to stir about halfway through the cooking time to move the cooked edges toward the center. Baked goods, such as English muffins and bread, are crisper and tastier when toasted before adding a topping. When heating sandwich-type items, cover or wrap them in paper towels to hold in the heat and absorb excess moisture. Many breakfast meats microwave nicely, but the dishes are sometimes difficult to clean. Just line the meat dishes or racks with paper toweling and cleanup will be much easier.

There are many other ways to use the microwave to simplify breakfast preparation. Thaw frozen concentrated juice for easier mixing with water. Soften refrigerated butter for easier spreading. Warm syrup and honey always taste better and can often be heated right in the serving containers. Frozen bread and muffins thaw easily in the microwave. When day-old bakery items are on sale, stock up and freeze them. Then thaw and freshen them with a few seconds in the microwave. Bacon slices are often difficult to separate. A few seconds in the microwave makes them much easier to handle. And, of course, many of our morning beverages are super when heated right in the serving mug.

Try these day-starter menus and have a nutritous, hassle-free breakfast that is high in good nutrition. Use the menus as a guide, but also feel free to vary them and include your own favorite creations. A different bread or fruit or a change of meat can quickly create a new entree or menu. Children will love to help with some of the simpler preparations. And you'll appreciate the variety possible and feel good about the fact that your family is eating a meal that will get them off to a good start!

Oatmeal is a breakfast favorite of many. It is super-easy to prepare in the microwave and goes well with the Orange Whip at only 250 calories total. If preparing a single serving, make the oatmeal right in the serving dish.

MENU
BANANA-DATE OATMEAL
ORANGE WHIP

TIME GUIDE
About 15 minutes ahead:
Prepare Orange Whip.
Prepare Banana-Date Oatmeal.

BANANA-DATE OATMEAL

**About 2 servings,
175 calories each**

Fresh and dried fruit add sweetness to hot cereal, so additional sugar may not be necessary.

1½ **cups water**

¼ **teaspoon salt**

2 **tablespoons chopped dates**

⅔ **cup quick-cooking rolled oats**

½ **banana, sliced**

Skim milk

1. Combine water, salt, dates, and rolled oats in 4-cup microwave-safe measure.
2. MICROWAVE (high), uncovered, 4–5 minutes or until mixture boils, stirring once. Let stand 2–3 minutes. Stir in banana. Add milk until desired consistency.

TIP

● Raisins can be substituted for chopped dates.

ORANGE WHIP

**About 4 servings,
75 calories each**

Buttermilk is the surprise ingredient in this refreshing drink.

2 **tablespoons sugar**

¼ **cup water**

1½ **cups buttermilk**

1 **teaspoon grated orange peel**

1 **orange, peeled and sectioned**

6 **ice cubes**

1. MICROWAVE (high) sugar and water in uncovered 1-cup microwave-safe measure 1½–2 minutes or until mixture boils and sugar is dissolved.
2. Combine buttermilk, orange peel and sections, and sugar syrup in blender or food processor container. Blend until smooth. Add ice cubes, one at a time, and process until frothy.

If you enjoy Mexican flavors, you'll want to try this breakfast menu with only 270 calories. The drink is made the night before to help make the morning preparation super-quick.

MENU
MEXICAN EGG ROLL-UPS
ZIPPY TOMATO DRINK

TIME GUIDE
Night before:
Prepare Zippy Tomato Drink, except for garnish.

About 10 minutes ahead:
Prepare Mexican Egg Roll-Ups.
Pour drink into glasses and garnish.

MEXICAN EGG ROLL-UPS

**About 4 servings,
250 calories each**

Scrambled eggs and cheese are rolled inside flour tortillas and topped with a zesty tomato mixture for this south-of-the-border breakfast idea.

3 eggs

3 tablespoons water

⅛ teaspoon hot pepper sauce

4 8-inch flour tortillas

⅓ cup shredded cheddar cheese

1 medium tomato, chopped

2 green onions, sliced (including tops)

¼ cup chunky taco sauce

1. Beat eggs, water, and hot pepper sauce in 1-quart microwave-safe mixing bowl until light.

2. MICROWAVE (high), uncovered, 2–2½ minutes or until just about set, stirring twice. Place tortillas on flat surface. Divide egg mixture among tortillas; spread slightly. Sprinkle each with cheese. Roll up tortillas with egg inside. Place on microwave-safe serving plate. Cover with waxed paper.

3. MICROWAVE (high) 2–2½ minutes or until hot, rotating plate once. Sprinkle with remaining ingredients.

TIP

- For an easy breakfast on the go, spoon ingredients inside each tortilla. Fold up bottom quarter of tortilla; roll up tortilla and place on napkin. MICROWAVE each tortilla 20–30 seconds or until hot and then take it with you.

ZIPPY TOMATO DRINK

**About 4 servings,
20 calories each**

Worcestershire sauce, celery salt, and cayenne pepper add zip to this chilled tomato beverage.

2 cups tomato juice

⅓ cup water

1 teaspoon sugar

1 teaspoon instant beef bouillon

¼ teaspoon celery salt

1 teaspoon lemon juice

Dash Worcestershire sauce

Dash cayenne pepper

4 celery sticks, about 5 inches long

1. Chill tomato juice. Combine water, sugar, bouillon, and celery salt in 1-cup microwave-safe measure.

2. MICROWAVE (high), uncovered, 1½–2 minutes or until boiling. Stir to dissolve bouillon. Mix in lemon juice, Worcestershire sauce, and pepper. Blend with chilled juice. Refrigerate until served. Garnish with celery sticks.

TIP

● Celery seed can be substituted for celery salt.

Breakfast for two is ready in just 10 minutes. What a cheerful way to start the day at just 320 calories per serving.

MENU
HAM AND EGG SANDWICH CUPS
CINNAMON COFFEE

TIME GUIDE
About 10 minutes ahead:
Prepare Ham and Egg Sandwich Cups, steps 1 and 2.
Prepare Cinnamon Coffee.
Complete sandwich cups, steps 3 and 4.

HAM AND EGG SANDWICH CUPS   2 servings, 270 calories each

Toast cups make individual holders for a delicious scrambled egg mixture.

2 slices whole grain bread

1 tablespoon margarine

2 eggs

2 tablespoons water

½ cup chopped cooked ham

¼ teaspoon snipped chives

2 tablespoons shredded cheddar cheese

1. Trim crusts from bread. Gently press slices into two 5-ounce microwave-safe custard cups. Set aside.

2. MICROWAVE (high) margarine in uncovered microwave-safe dish 15–20 seconds or until softened. Brush over bread, including edges.

3. MICROWAVE (high), uncovered, 1–1½ minutes or until bread is slightly dried. Beat together eggs and water; mix in ham and chives. Divide mixture between cups.

4. MICROWAVE (high), uncovered, 2–3 minutes or until just about set. Top with cheese.

TIP

• The cholesterol-free egg substitute can be used for eggs. Use ½ cup.

CINNAMON COFFEE

2 servings,
50 calories each

Cinnamon candies add a nice flavor to this coffee. It can also be served with whipped topping for a delightful dessert beverage.

2 cups water

2 teaspoons red hot cinnamon candies

2 teaspoons instant coffee crystals

2 tablespoons frozen whipped topping, thawed (optional)

1. Divide water and candies between two microwave-safe mugs.

2. MICROWAVE (high), uncovered, 5–5½ minutes or until candies are dissolved. Stir in instant coffee. If desired, garnish with whipped topping.

Plenty of fruit and fiber make this 265-calorie breakfast menu a just-right combination. It's sure to wake up sleepy appetites.

MENU
YOGURT-FRUIT BOWL
APPLE-BRAN COFFEECAKE

TIME GUIDE
About 30 minutes ahead:
Prepare Yogurt-Fruit Bowl, steps 1 and 2.
Prepare Apple-Bran Coffeecake.
Complete fruit bowl, step 3.

YOGURT-FRUIT BOWL

**4 servings,
110 calories each**

This combination of fresh and canned fruit has a creamy yogurt glaze.

1 8-ounce can sliced peaches

1 teaspoon cornstarch

½ cup vanilla yogurt

1 kiwifruit, peeled and sliced

1 medium banana, peeled and sliced

1. Drain juice from peaches into 2-cup microwave-safe measure. Blend in cornstarch.

2. MICROWAVE (high), uncovered, 1–1¼ minutes or until mixture boils and thickens, stirring once. Cool.

3. Stir in yogurt, peach slices, kiwifruit, and banana.

TIPS

- Other combinations of fruit can be used. Select colors and flavors that complement each other.

- Lite fruits can be substituted; calories will be reduced to about 85 per serving.

APPLE-BRAN COFFEECAKE

**About 8 servings,
155 calories each**

Start the day with this nutritious coffeecake studded with bits of apple and served warm from the microwave.

½ cup buttermilk or sour milk

⅓ cup all-bran cereal

¼ cup packed brown sugar

¼ cup cooking oil

½ teaspoon vanilla

1 egg

¾ cup unsifted all-purpose flour

½ teaspoon soda

¼ teaspoon baking powder

¼ teaspoon salt

1 apple, peeled and quartered

⅛ teaspoon ground cinnamon

1 teaspoon sugar

1. Combine buttermilk and cereal; mix well. Blend in brown sugar, oil, vanilla, and egg. Add flour, soda, baking powder, and salt; mix just until moistened. Reserve one quarter of the apple for top; chop remaining apple and stir into batter. Spread in 8-inch round microwave-safe baking dish. Slice remaining apple thinly; arrange spoke-fashion on batter. Mix together cinnamon and sugar; sprinkle over apples.

2. MICROWAVE (high), uncovered, 4½–5½ minutes or until no longer doughy, rotating dish once. Let stand 5 minutes. Cut into wedges to serve.

TIP

● A fresh peach or ¾ cup fresh blueberries can be substituted for apple.

"Fast and easy" describes this 255-calorie meal. It is perfect for those hectic mornings when the family is in a rush to go to work or school.

MENU
WAFFLES WITH PEACH SAUCE
CANADIAN BACON

TIME GUIDE
About 15 minutes ahead:
Prepare Waffles with Peach Sauce, steps 1 and 2.
Prepare Canadian Bacon.
Complete waffles, steps 3 and 4.

WAFFLES WITH PEACH SAUCE

About 4 servings, 175 calories each

Warm peach sauce over waffles makes a quick breakfast.

1 8-ounce can sliced peaches

Water

2 teaspoons cornstarch

1 teaspoon lemon juice

⅛ teaspoon ground cinnamon

4 frozen waffles

1. Drain juice from peaches into 2-cup microwave-safe measure. Add water to make ⅔ cup. Blend in cornstarch, lemon juice, and cinnamon.

2. MICROWAVE (high), uncovered, 1¼–1½ minutes or until mixture boils and thickens, stirring once. Add peaches. Set aside. Arrange frozen waffles on microwave-safe serving plate.

3. MICROWAVE (high), uncovered, 1–1¼ minutes or until thawed. Top with peach sauce.

4. MICROWAVE (high), uncovered, 1½–2 minutes or until waffles are heated.

TIPS

- If heating a single serving, decrease time in step 3 to 15–30 seconds and in step 4 to 30–45 seconds.

- Also use peach sauce on pancakes or your own homemade waffles. Omit heating in step 4 when the pancakes or waffles are freshly prepared.

CANADIAN BACON

**About 4 servings,
80 calories each**

Precooked meats such as Canadian bacon heat nicely in the microwave.

8 ounces Canadian bacon

1. Cut bacon into thin slices. Arrange on microwave-safe serving plate. Cover with waxed paper.
2. MICROWAVE (high) 2½–3 minutes or until heated. Let stand, covered, a few minutes.

Weekends mean more time to prepare and eat a leisurely breakfast or brunch. Add toast or bagels to this 255-calorie menu, and your morning meal is complete.

MENU
MORNING FRITTATA
SPICED ORANGE TEA

TIME GUIDE
About 30 minutes ahead:
Prepare Morning Frittata, steps 1–3.
Prepare Spiced Orange Tea.
Complete frittata, step 4.

MORNING FRITTATA

**About 4 servings,
170 calories each**

This hearty combination of bacon, potatoes, and eggs will help get your day off to a good start.

3 **slices bacon**

2 **green onions, sliced
(including tops)**

6 **ounces frozen hash browns
(½ 12-ounce package)**

4 **eggs**

2 **tablespoons water**

4–5 **drops hot pepper sauce**

¼ **teaspoon salt**

Green pepper strips

¼ **cup shredded cheddar
cheese**

1. Cut bacon into small pieces; place in 9-inch microwave-safe pie plate. Add onions. Cover with paper towel.

2. MICROWAVE (high) 2½–3 minutes or until bacon is crisp. Drain fat, reserving 1 tablespoon in dish. Add frozen hash browns. Cover with plastic wrap.

3. MICROWAVE (high) 5–6 minutes or until potatoes are thawed, stirring twice. Beat together eggs, water, pepper sauce, and salt. Stir into potatoes. Garnish with green pepper strips. Cover with plastic wrap.

4. MICROWAVE (high) 2½–3½ minutes or until eggs are set. Sprinkle with cheese.

SPICED ORANGE TEA

Prepare extra servings of this in the morning and then enjoy it throughout the day.

3 cups water

1 cup orange juice

¼ cup sugar

¼ cup lemon juice

2 tea bags

2 cinnamon sticks

12 whole cloves

1. Combine all ingredients in 1-quart microwave-safe pitcher or teapot.

2. MICROWAVE (high), uncovered, 9–10 minutes or until steaming hot (190° F). Let stand 5 minutes. Remove tea bags, cinnamon sticks, and cloves. Serve hot or iced.

This morning meal of fancy scrambled eggs and glazed fresh fruit has only 265 calories. The fruit can be prepared the night before; just wait to add the apple until shortly before serving time.

MENU
CHEESY EGGS WITH BACON
GLAZED FRUIT BOWL

TIME GUIDE
About 20 minutes ahead:
Prepare Cheesy Eggs with Bacon, steps 1-3.
Prepare Glazed Fruit Bowl.
Complete eggs, steps 4 and 5.

CHEESY EGGS WITH BACON

**About 4 servings,
195 calories each**

Get your day off to a good start with this combination of eggs, bacon, and cheese.

2 slices bacon

6 eggs

6 tablespoons water

1 tablespoon snipped chives

½ teaspoon salt

⅛ teaspoon pepper

½ cup (2 ounces) shredded cheddar cheese

1. Place bacon on paper towel–lined microwave-safe meat rack or paper plate. Cover with paper towel.

2. MICROWAVE (high) 1½–2 minutes or until crisp. Set aside.

3. Combine eggs, water, chives, salt, and pepper in 1½-quart microwave-safe casserole. Beat with fork until blended. Cover with casserole lid.

4. MICROWAVE (high) 4–5 minutes or until eggs are just about set, stirring twice. Sprinkle with cheese and crumbled bacon. Cover.

5. MICROWAVE (high) 30–60 seconds or until cheese is melted.

GLAZED FRUIT BOWL

**About 4 servings,
70 calories each**

Add or substitute other seasonal fresh fruit in this easy combination.

1 orange, peeled and chopped

1 apple, cored and chopped

1 cup seedless grapes

2 tablespoons apple jelly

⅛ teaspoon ground cinnamon

1. Combine fruit in 3- to 4-cup serving dish. Set aside.

2. MICROWAVE (high) jelly in uncovered 1-cup microwave-safe measure 45–60 seconds or until melted. Stir in cinnamon. Pour over fruit; mix lightly to coat.

TIP

- A tablespoon of honey can be substituted for apple jelly.

This 200-calorie menu makes a quick day starter when the muffin batter is prepared ahead and kept in the refrigerator. Vary your meal by combining the muffins with some of the other fruit suggestions in this chapter.

MENU
SUGAR-GLAZED GRAPEFRUIT
TOP-OF-THE-MORNING BRAN MUFFINS

TIME GUIDE
About 20 minutes ahead:
Prepare Top-of-the-Morning Bran Muffins.
Prepare Sugar-Glazed Grapefruit.

SUGAR-GLAZED GRAPEFRUIT

**4 servings,
70 calories each**

Warming grapefruit brings out the juicy flavor and allows the sugar to glaze the fruit.

2 grapefruit, halved

2 tablespoons brown sugar

*2 maraschino cherries, halved
(optional)*

1. Remove seeds from grapefruit halves. Cut around sections to loosen. Place on one large or four small microwave-safe plates. Top each half with ½ tablespoon brown sugar. Garnish each with cherry half.

2. MICROWAVE (high), uncovered, 2–3 minutes or until grapefruit are heated and sugar is melted.

TOP-OF-THE-MORNING BRAN MUFFINS

**About 12 muffins,
130 calories each**

*This make-ahead bran muffin batter can be refrigerated and then microwaved any time
of the day for a nutritious snack or meal accompaniment.*

1 cup all-bran cereal

1 cup buttermilk or sour milk

¼ cup sugar

¼ cup cooking oil

1 egg

1 cup unsifted all-purpose flour

1 teaspoon baking powder

½ teaspoon soda

¼ teaspoon salt

1 tablespoon sugar

¼ teaspoon ground cinnamon

1. Combine bran cereal and buttermilk in 1-quart microwave-safe mixing bowl; mix lightly.

2. MICROWAVE (high), uncovered, 2–2½ minutes or until liquid is absorbed. Mix in sugar, oil, and egg. Add flour, baking powder, soda, and salt; stir just until moistened.

3. Spoon batter into 12 paper-lined microwave-safe muffin cups, filling cups half full. Combine sugar and cinnamon; sprinkle each muffin with mixture.

4. MICROWAVE (high) 6 muffins at a time, uncovered, 2–2½ minutes or until no longer doughy, rotating pan once.

TIP

- Extra batter can be refrigerated for up to 3 weeks and used as needed. Increase cooking time to 2¼–2¾ minutes.

Frozen pancakes help to make this 305-calorie menu quick and easy to prepare. You can vary it by using your own ready-prepared pancakes or French toast.

MENU
BLUEBERRY SHORTSTACKS
MOCHA COFFEE

TIME GUIDE
About 10 minutes ahead:
Prepare Blueberry Shortstacks, steps 1–3.
Prepare Mocha Coffee.
Complete shortstacks, steps 4 and 5.

BLUEBERRY SHORTSTACKS

**2 servings,
280 calories each**

A light blueberry syrup tops frozen pancakes. Use the ready-to-eat frozen pancakes or freeze extras from your favorite recipe.

**1 cup frozen unsweetened
  blueberries**

2 tablespoons sugar

1 teaspoon cornstarch

1 teaspoon water

1 teaspoon margarine

4 frozen pancakes

1. Combine blueberries and sugar in 1-cup microwave-safe measure.

2. MICROWAVE (high), uncovered, 2–2½ minutes or until berries are thawed, stirring once. Combine cornstarch and water in 2-cup microwave-safe measure. Drain juices from berries into measure; mix well.

3. MICROWAVE (high), uncovered, 1–1½ minutes or until mixture boils and thickens, stirring once. Stir in margarine. Add berries; mix gently.

4. Stack two pancakes on each of two microwave-safe plates. Divide berry mixture between the two plates.

5. MICROWAVE (high) one plate at a time, uncovered, 1½–2 minutes or until hot, rotating plate once.

TIP

● Frozen French toast can be substituted for pancakes. Calories will be about the same.

MOCHA COFFEE

About 2 servings, 25 calories each

Cocoa, milk, and a dash of cinnamon give coffee a new flavor.

½ cup water

2 teaspoons sugar

1 teaspoon unsweetened cocoa

¾ cup water

2 teaspoons instant coffee crystals

2 tablespoons skim milk

Ground cinnamon

1. Combine ½ cup water, sugar, and cocoa in 2-cup microwave-safe measure.

2. MICROWAVE (high), uncovered, 1–1½ minutes or until mixture boils, stirring once. Stir in ¾ cup water, coffee crystals, and milk.

3. MICROWAVE (high), uncovered, 1½–2 minutes or until steaming hot, stirring once. Sprinkle with cinnamon.

EASY STRAWBERRY JAM

About 2 cups,
15 calories/tablespoon

Flavored gelatin is the base for this lower-calorie, tasty jam.

2 cups sliced fresh strawberries

½ cup sugar

1 3-ounce package sugar-free strawberry-flavored gelatin

1 cup cold water

1. Combine strawberries and sugar in 2-quart microwave-safe mixing bowl. Mix well and let stand 10 minutes.
2. MICROWAVE (high), uncovered, 6–7 minutes or until mixture boils, stirring once.
3. Stir in gelatin; continue to stir for 2 minutes. Blend in water. Pour into sterilized jars. Refrigerate for 2–3 weeks or freeze for longer storage.

TIP

- Raspberries and raspberry-flavored gelatin can be substituted, or try peaches with raspberry-flavored gelatin.

LITE MAPLE SYRUP

About ¾ cup,
25 calories/tablespoon

Here is a homemade maple-flavored syrup to serve over French toast, waffles, or pancakes.

½ cup apple juice

2 teaspoons cornstarch

⅓ cup packed brown sugar

¼ cup water

¼ teaspoon maple flavoring

1. Combine juice, cornstarch, brown sugar, and water in 2-cup microwave-safe measure.
2. MICROWAVE (high), uncovered, 2–3 minutes or until mixture boils and thickens slightly, stirring once. Stir in flavoring. Store in refrigerator.

TIP

- To reheat refrigerated syrup, MICROWAVE 45–60 seconds.

CHAPTER
3
FAMILY MEALS

In this chapter of family-type dinners, you'll find a variety of meals from which to choose. We have included dishes as basic as macaroni and cheese and pizza as well as specialty dishes such as Moo Goo Gai Pan and Lemony Shrimp Fajitas.

The eating trend today is toward lighter meals, and we have taken familiar favorites and lightened them by using more vegetables, less fat, and reduced amounts of red-meat protein. The menus in this chapter were planned to be the main meal of the day, providing flavorful, satisfying dinners for 190 to 450 calories per meal. These calories are based only on the recipes included, so the addition of other accompaniments will increase the total calories.

As you page through the menus, you will see that most yield four to five servings, and many meals are special enough for company fare. For other family-type meals, be sure to check Chapter 6, "Quick and Easy Meals," Chapter 7, "Make-Ahead Meals," and Chapter 8, "Freezer Meals." And, if you are cooking for one or two, you'll find many smaller family meal ideas in Chapter 5, "Meals for One or Two."

While some of the recipes in this chapter are very easy, others require more time to complete. In many cases, we've suggested steps that can be done the night before or early in the day to ease the last-minute preparation. You can always select accompaniments from another menu to make the timing fit your schedule.

Family meals do not need to be the same day after day, nor do they have to be laden with calories. We are sure you will enjoy the variety as well as the delicious results you can achieve with the suggested menus and recipes in this chapter.

Try this menu, and you'll discover that fish and fresh vegetables cook beautifully in the microwave. The preparation is quick, too, taking only about 40 minutes for this 335-calorie meal.

MENU
SOLE OSCAR
DILLY NEW POTATOES

TIME GUIDE
About 40 minutes ahead:
Prepare Dilly New Potatoes, steps 1 and 2.
Prepare Sole Oscar.
Complete potatoes, step 3.

SOLE OSCAR

**About 4 servings,
150 calories each**

Fish and fresh asparagus team together in this lite, easy meal.

3 green onions, sliced

1 cup (4 ounces) sliced fresh mushrooms

1 pound asparagus spears, trimmed

2 teaspoons instant chicken bouillon

¼ cup water

1 tablespoon margarine

1 pound sole fillets

Salt

2 teaspoons cornstarch

1 tablespoon lemon juice

Lemon wedges (optional)

1. Combine onions, mushrooms, asparagus, bouillon, water, and margarine in 12- by 8-inch microwave-safe baking dish. Cover with plastic wrap.

2. MICROWAVE (high) 3–4 minutes or until asparagus is almost tender. Arrange fish on the vegetables; sprinkle lightly with salt. Cover with plastic wrap.

3. MICROWAVE (high) 4–5 minutes or until fish flakes apart easily. Transfer fish and asparagus to serving platter and cover with foil. Mix cornstarch with lemon juice. Stir into remaining vegetables and sauce in pan.

4. MICROWAVE (high), uncovered, 1–2 minutes or until mixture boils and thickens, stirring once. Pour sauce over fish and asparagus. Garnish with lemon wedges.

TIP

- If serving platter is microwave-safe and will fit under baking dish in oven, place it there during cooking to warm the platter.

DILLY NEW POTATOES

**About 4 servings,
85 calories each**

Fresh new potatoes taste so good that only a small amount of margarine is needed to enhance the flavor.

**8-12 small new potatoes (about
1½ pounds)**
¼ cup water
1 tablespoon margarine
½ teaspoon salt
¼ teaspoon dried dill weed
⅛ teaspoon pepper

1. Scrub potatoes and cut thin strip of peel from center of each. Place in 1-quart microwave-safe casserole. Add water. Cover with casserole lid.

2. MICROWAVE (high) 7–8 minutes or until just about tender, rearranging once. Let stand a few minutes. Drain. Add margarine, salt, dill weed, and pepper; mix lightly. Cover.

3. MICROWAVE (high) 1–2 minutes or until margarine is melted.

This colorful 305-calorie menu is appropriate for a special family dinner or when entertaining guests. If you are on a limited budget, omit the shrimp and substitute a less expensive seafood. To simplify last-minute preparation, get the vegetables ready several hours ahead of time.

MENU
SHRIMP PRIMAVERA
GARLIC STICKS

TIME GUIDE
About 45 minutes ahead:
Prepare Shrimp Primavera.
Prepare Garlic Sticks.

SHRIMP PRIMAVERA

About 4 servings, 285 calories each

This attractive pasta dish is enhanced with shrimp.

6 cups hot water

½ teaspoon salt

6 ounces linguine noodles

1 cup cauliflower pieces

1 cup (4 ounces) sliced fresh mushrooms

1 cup thinly sliced carrots

1 cup broccoli pieces

½ cup sliced red pepper strips

2 tablespoons water

1 12-ounce package frozen cooked shrimp, rinsed and drained

½ cup evaporated skim milk

¼ cup grated Parmesan cheese

¼ teaspoon salt

⅛ teaspoon dried basil leaves

Dash pepper

1. MICROWAVE (high) 6 cups hot water and ½ teaspoon salt in uncovered 2-quart microwave-safe mixing bowl 7–8 minutes or until steaming hot. Break linguine into about 3-inch lengths; add to water.

2. MICROWAVE (high), uncovered, 8–9 minutes or until tender, stirring twice. Let stand 5 minutes. Drain and rinse in cold water. Set aside.

3. Combine cauliflower, mushrooms, carrots, broccoli, red pepper, and 2 tablespoons water in 3-quart microwave-safe casserole. Cover with casserole lid.

4. MICROWAVE (high) 7–9 minutes or until tender. Drain. Add noodles, shrimp, milk, Parmesan cheese, ¼ teaspoon salt, basil, and pepper.

5. MICROWAVE (high), uncovered, 2–4 minutes or until heated through.

GARLIC STICKS

Use leftover bread crusts for this easy version of garlic toast.

1 tablespoon margarine

⅛ teaspoon garlic powder

⅛ teaspoon paprika

2 slices bread, preferably crusty ends

2 tablespoons grated Parmesan cheese

1. MICROWAVE (high) margarine in uncovered 1-cup microwave-safe measure 20–30 seconds or until melted. Stir in garlic and paprika. Brush on top side of bread; sprinkle with Parmesan cheese. Cut each slice into 6 sticks. Place on microwave-safe plate.

2. MICROWAVE (high), uncovered, 2–2½ minutes or until toasted, rotating plate once.

If your family likes southwestern-style cooking, treat them to this menu featuring fajitas. A popular dish at Mexican restaurants, they are easy to prepare in your microwave. Flavorful rice completes this 310-calorie meal.

MENU
LEMONY SHRIMP FAJITAS
GUACAMOLE
MEXICAN RICE

TIME GUIDE
About 40 minutes ahead:
Prepare Guacamole.
Prepare Mexican Rice.
Prepare Lemony Shrimp Fajitas.

LEMONY SHRIMP FAJITAS

**4 fajitas,
155 calories each**

These are so quick and easy that you may want to serve them often for a meal or snack.

¾ cup thinly sliced green pepper

3 green onions, sliced

1 clove garlic, minced

½ teaspoon chili powder

¼ teaspoon ground cumin

1 6-ounce package frozen cooked shrimp, rinsed and drained

1 medium tomato, chopped

½ lemon, cut into 8 pieces

4 flour tortillas

1 cup shredded lettuce

Guacamole (see recipe below)

Salsa (optional)

1. Combine green pepper, onions, garlic, chili powder, and cumin in 1-quart microwave-safe casserole. Cover with casserole lid.

2. MICROWAVE (high) 1½–2 minutes or until green pepper and onions are tender. Add shrimp, tomato, and lemon. Cover.

3. MICROWAVE (high) 1½–2½ minutes or until shrimp are heated. Remove lemon pieces. Wrap tortillas in plastic wrap.

4. MICROWAVE (high) 30 seconds or until warm. Top each tortilla with ¼ cup lettuce and ¼ of the shrimp mixture. Fold up edges with the filling in the center. Serve with guacamole and salsa.

TIP

• Sliced cooked beef or chicken can be substituted for shrimp. Use about 1½ cups.

GUACAMOLE

**About 1 cup,
20 calories/tablespoon**

This guacamole uses low-fat cottage cheese to reduce the calories.

1   **medium avocado, peeled and
    chopped**

¼   **cup low-fat cottage cheese**

2   **tablespoons chopped onion**

2   **tablespoons chopped tomato**

1   **tablespoon lemon juice**

1   **small clove garlic**

¼   **teaspoon salt**

1. Combine all ingredients in blender or food
   processor container. Blend until smooth. Serve
   with Lemony Shrimp Fajitas or other favorite
   Mexican foods.

MEXICAN RICE

**About 4 servings,
135 calories each**

A tasty and colorful way to serve rice for any meal.

¼   **cup chopped red pepper**

¼   **cup chopped green onion**

1   **clove garlic, minced**

¼   **teaspoon dried basil leaves**

2   **teaspoons instant chicken
    bouillon**

1½ **cups water**

¾   **cup uncooked long-grain
    white rice**

1. Combine all ingredients in 1-quart microwave-
   safe casserole. Cover with casserole lid.
2. MICROWAVE (high) 5–6 minutes or until
   mixture boils. Then MICROWAVE (low—30%)
   12–14 minutes or until rice is tender. Let stand 5
   minutes; fluff with fork.

TIP

• To use full power instead of the lower power setting in step 2, MICROWAVE 3 minutes
  and let stand 4 minutes, twice.

This 265-calorie menu of fish roll-ups and vegetable is perfectly suited to microwave cooking. Fish and vegetables are some of the best microwaved foods. The menu is special enough for company meals, too.

MENU
FISH FILLET ROLL-UPS
SESAME BROCCOLI AND CARROTS

TIME GUIDE
About 45 minutes ahead:
Prepare Fish Fillet Roll-Ups, step 1.
Prepare Sesame Broccoli and Carrots.
Complete fish, steps 2–4.

FISH FILLET ROLL-UPS

About 4 servings, 190 calories each

Mushrooms and onions are tucked inside fish fillets, then topped with a light and delicious sauce.

2 **cups (8 ounces) sliced fresh mushrooms**

3 **green onions, sliced (including tops)**

4 **fish fillets (about 1 pound)**

¼ **teaspoon salt**

¼ **cup dry white wine**

¼ **cup skim milk**

1 **tablespoon flour**

¼ **cup shredded Swiss cheese**

1 **tablespoon snipped fresh parsley**

1. MICROWAVE (high) mushrooms and onions in uncovered 2-cup microwave-safe measure 2–3 minutes or until tender. Drain.

2. Place fillets on flat surface and sprinkle with salt. Top with mushroom and onion mixture. Roll up each fillet, starting at narrow end. Place seam side down in 8-inch round microwave-safe baking dish. Pour wine over fish. Cover with plastic wrap.

3. MICROWAVE (high) 4–4½ minutes or until fish flakes apart easily, rotating dish once. Set aside. Combine milk and flour in 1-cup microwave-safe measure. Drain juices from fish into milk mixture; mix well.

4. MICROWAVE (high), uncovered, 1½–2 minutes or until mixture boils and thickens, stirring once. Pour sauce over fillets. Top with cheese and parsley.

TIP

● Apple juice or water can be substituted for wine.

SESAME BROCCOLI AND CARROTS

Carrots and broccoli team together in this flavorful dish.

2 cups sliced carrots (½ inch thick)

2 cups broccoli pieces

2 tablespoons water

1 tablespoon margarine

2 teaspoons sesame seed

⅛ teaspoon salt

⅛ teaspoon dried tarragon leaves

1. Combine carrots, broccoli, and water in 1-quart microwave-safe casserole. Cover loosely with casserole lid.

2. MICROWAVE (high) 8–10 minutes or until tender. Drain. Add margarine, sesame seed, salt, and tarragon; mix lightly.

This versatile pork dinner of 315 calories is ready in about an hour. When you need more carefree preparation, make the carrots the day or night before.

MENU
MANDARIN PORK MEDALLIONS
CARROT COINS

TIME GUIDE
About 2 hours ahead:
Prepare Carrot Coins.

About 1 hour ahead:
Prepare Mandarin Pork Medallions.

MANDARIN PORK MEDALLIONS

About 4 servings, 265 calories each

Pork tenderloin is delicious cooked in the microwave and is ready in minimal time, too. Your family will surely love it.

½ *cup fresh orange juice*

2 *teaspoons cornstarch*

½ *teaspoon Dijon mustard*

1 *tablespoon orange marmalade*

2 *tablespoons dry sherry*

1 *10-ounce can mandarin oranges, drained*

¾ *pound pork tenderloin*

¼ *teaspoon crushed dried thyme leaves*

1. Combine orange juice, cornstarch, mustard, and marmalade in 2-cup microwave-safe measure.

2. MICROWAVE (high), uncovered, 1½–2 minutes or until mixture boils and thickens, stirring once. Stir in sherry and oranges. Set aside.

3. Place tenderloin in 10- by 6-inch microwave-safe baking dish. Rub thyme into pork. Brush with part of the sauce. Cover with waxed paper.

4. MICROWAVE (high) 7–9 minutes or until pork is done (160° F), turning once and brushing with additional sauce. Let stand 5 minutes.

5. Cut tenderloin across grain into thin slices; arrange on microwave-safe serving platter. Stir drippings into sauce; spoon over pork.

6. MICROWAVE (high), uncovered, 1–2 minutes or until heated.

CARROT COINS

These slightly tangy carrots are served chilled and add color to any meal.

2 cups sliced carrots

2 tablespoons water

¼ cup lite Italian dressing

1 tablespoon catsup

1 teaspoon sugar

2 tablespoons chopped green
pepper

1. Combine carrots and water in 20-ounce microwave-safe casserole. Cover with plastic wrap.

2. MICROWAVE (high), 3–4 minutes or until carrots are just about tender. Let stand a few minutes. Drain.

3. Combine dressing, catsup, sugar, and green pepper in 1-cup measure. Pour over carrots; mix well. Chill.

You'll enjoy the Greek flair of this meal of 405 calories. Even though it sounds special, it takes only 30 minutes. The moussaka reheats well, making it ideal for latecomers, too.

MENU
GREEN BEAN MOUSSAKA
CHEESY WEDGES

TIME GUIDE
About 30 minutes ahead:
Prepare Green Bean Moussaka.
Prepare Cheesy Wedges.

GREEN BEAN MOUSSAKA

About 4 servings, 315 calories each

Try green beans in this unique version of a Greek favorite.

1 pound lean ground beef

1 small onion, chopped

1 clove garlic, minced

1 16-ounce can cut green beans, drained

1 8-ounce can tomato sauce

¼ teaspoon ground cinnamon

1 egg, slightly beaten

¾ cup low-fat cottage cheese

1 tablespoon grated Parmesan cheese

1 tablespoon snipped fresh parsley

1. Crumble beef into 8- by 8-inch microwave-safe baking dish. Mix in onion and garlic.

2. MICROWAVE (high), uncovered, 5–6 minutes or until meat is no longer pink, stirring once. Drain.

3. Stir in green beans, tomato sauce, and cinnamon. Mix egg and cottage cheese; spread over hot mixture. Sprinkle with Parmesan cheese and parsley. Cover with plastic wrap.

4. MICROWAVE (medium-high—70%) 10–12 minutes or until hot and bubbly, rotating dish once. Let stand 5 minutes. Cut into squares to serve.

TIPS

- To use full power in step 4, MICROWAVE 5 minutes, rotating dish once. Let stand 5 minutes. Then MICROWAVE 3–4 minutes longer, rotating dish once.

- Ground lamb can be substituted for beef.

CHEESY WEDGES

**About 4 servings,
90 calories each**

Pita pockets are filled with mozzarella cheese and cut into wedges. Serve them often as an accompaniment or appetizer.

1 6-inch pita bread

¼ cup shredded mozzarella cheese

1 tablespoon margarine

½ teaspoon salad seasoning (Salad Supreme)

1. Carefully slit open pita bread to make 2 rounds. Place one half on microwave-safe plate. Sprinkle with cheese. Top with remaining half of bread; set aside.

2. MICROWAVE (high) margarine in 1-cup microwave-safe measure 20–30 seconds or until melted. Stir in salad seasoning. Brush on pocket bread.

3. MICROWAVE (high), uncovered, 1–1½ minutes or until cheese is melted. Cut into 16 wedges.

Can a meal be hearty, yet lite? This one proves it can with a flavorful dinner of soup, fruit salad, and muffins that adds up to only 425 calories. The Time Guide suggests preparing the foods just before serving, but the soup is delicious reheated. Prepare it in advance, then just reheat for serving.

MENU
BEEFY MEATBALL MINESTRONE
CHEESY PEACH HALVES
CORN BREAD MUFFINS

TIME GUIDE
About 40 minutes ahead:
Prepare Beefy Meatball Minestrone.
Prepare Cheesy Peach Halves.
Prepare Corn Bread Muffins.
Reheat soup, if necessary.

BEEFY MEATBALL MINESTRONE
About 6 servings, 215 calories each

Meatballs are added to this hearty Italian soup. You'll want to enjoy this often on cold winter days.

1 pound lean ground beef

1 egg

1 tablespoon dry bread crumbs

1 tablespoon grated Parmesan cheese

¾ teaspoon salt

⅛ teaspoon pepper

2 medium carrots, diced

1 medium onion, chopped

1 clove garlic, minced

1 zucchini, chopped

1 medium tomato, chopped

½ cup uncooked spaghetti (about 3 ounces), broken into 1½-inch pieces

3 teaspoons instant beef bouillon

1. Combine ground beef, egg, bread crumbs, cheese, ¾ teaspoon salt, and ⅛ teaspoon pepper; mix lightly. Form into ¾-inch meatballs and place in 3-quart microwave-safe casserole. Cover with casserole lid.

2. MICROWAVE (high) 5–6 minutes or until meatballs are cooked, rearranging once. Drain. Add remaining ingredients except spinach. Cover.

3. MICROWAVE (high) 14–16 minutes or until vegetables and spaghetti are tender. Add spinach; cover.

4. MICROWAVE (high) 2–3 minutes or until spinach is tender. Let stand 5 minutes.

½ **teaspoon salt**

½ **teaspoon dried basil leaves**

⅛ **teaspoon pepper**

2 **cups hot water**

8 **ounces fresh spinach, chopped (about 6 cups)**

TIP

● Half a 10-ounce package frozen chopped spinach can be substituted for the fresh. Increase time in step 4 to 3–4 minutes.

CHEESY PEACH HALVES

About 8 peaches, 110 calories each

A simple but nice salad that goes well with many main dishes.

1 **16-ounce can peach halves in fruit juice, drained**

   Lettuce or spinach leaves

3 **ounces Neufchâtel cheese**

1 **tablespoon grated Parmesan cheese**

1 **teaspoon skim milk**

Ground nutmeg

1. Arrange peach halves cut side up on lettuce or spinach leaves; set aside.

2. MICROWAVE (high) Neufchâtel cheese in small uncovered microwave-safe bowl 15–30 seconds or until softened. Stir until creamy. Blend in Parmesan cheese and milk. Spoon mixture evenly into peach halves. Sprinkle with nutmeg.

CORN BREAD MUFFINS

8 muffins, 100 calories each

Corn bread muffins can be enjoyed any time of the day. These are so moist there is no need to add butter—enjoy them plain or with a little honey.

2 **tablespoons margarine**

2 **tablespoons sugar**

1 **egg**

½ **cup buttermilk or sour milk**

½ **cup unsifted all-purpose flour**

⅓ **cup yellow cornmeal**

½ **teaspoon baking powder**

¼ **teaspoon salt**

⅛ **teaspoon soda**

3 **tablespoons cornflake crumbs**

1. MICROWAVE (high) margarine in microwave-safe mixing bowl 30–45 seconds or until melted.

2. Blend in sugar; beat in egg. Stir in buttermilk and remaining ingredients except cornflake crumbs, just until smooth. Sprinkle ½ teaspoon cornflake crumbs in bottom of each of 8 paper-lined microwave-safe muffin cups. Spoon batter into cups, filling cups half full. Sprinkle with remaining cornflake crumbs.

3. MICROWAVE (high) 6 muffins at a time, uncovered, 2–2½ minutes or until no longer doughy, rotating pan once. Repeat with remaining batter, MICROWAVING last 2 muffins about 1 minute.

This good and easy 400-calorie meal is everybody's favorite—pizza. Since special microwave accessories are necessary to get pizza crisp in the microwave, we cook the crust conventionally and then do the final heating in the microwave oven. A marinated vegetable salad completes the meal.

MENU
ALL-AMERICAN PIZZA
MARINATED GARDEN SALAD

TIME GUIDE
Day before or several hours ahead:
Prepare crusts for pizza, steps 1–3.
Prepare Marinated Garden Salad, steps 1 and 2.

About 30 minutes ahead:
Prepare pizza, steps 4 and 5.
Complete salad, step 3.

ALL-AMERICAN PIZZA

2 pizzas, about 8 slices each, 135 calories/piece

This pizza crust is best precooked in a conventional oven. Then use it to prepare quick pizzas in the microwave.

⅔ cup warm water

1 package active dry yeast

1 tablespoon cornmeal

½ teaspoon salt

1 tablespoon cooking oil

1½–1¾ cups unsifted all-purpose flour

Sauce

1 8-ounce can tomato sauce

1 teaspoon Italian seasoning

¼ cup chopped green pepper

Dash garlic powder

1. Add yeast to warm water in mixing bowl. Let stand a few minutes to soften. Blend in cornmeal, salt, and oil. Add ¾ cup flour. Beat well. Gradually add remaining flour to form a stiff dough. Turn onto floured surface. Knead until smooth, 2–3 minutes. Let dough stand, covered, about 5 minutes.

2. Preheat oven to 425° F. Divide dough in half. Roll out each half on ungreased baking sheet to a 10-inch circle (or size that will fit inside your microwave). Prick with fork.

3. Bake 10–12 minutes or until lightly browned. Transfer to cooling rack. When cool, wrap and store 2–3 days at room temperature or 2–3 months in freezer.

4. To prepare pizza, spread half the tomato sauce on each pizza crust. Sprinkle each with half the seasoning and green pepper. Sprinkle with garlic

¼ cup grated Parmesan
cheese

2 ounces thinly sliced
pepperoni

2 cups (8 ounces) shredded
mozzarella cheese

powder and Parmesan cheese. Arrange
pepperoni on each pizza; sprinkle each with half
the mozzarella cheese. Place each pizza on
cardboard circle or several layers of paper
toweling.

5. MICROWAVE (high) one pizza at a time,
uncovered, 4–5 minutes or until cheese is melted,
rotating once if necessary. Allow 2 slices per
serving.

TIPS

- For more topping, add 1 cup shredded zucchini, spinach, or mushrooms with
pepperoni on each pizza.

- Thinly sliced turkey franks or low-fat sausages can be substituted for all or part of
pepperoni.

MARINATED GARDEN SALAD

**About 8 servings,
130 calories each**

*Cauliflower and broccoli are partially cooked for a tender-crisp addition to this
marinated salad mixture. The vinegar is added just prior to serving since it often
bleaches green vegetables.*

1 medium head cauliflower

1 pound fresh broccoli

2 tablespoons water

½ cup salad oil

½ teaspoon salt

½ teaspoon oregano leaves

⅛ teaspoon pepper

1 clove garlic, minced

6 green onions, sliced

6-8 radishes, sliced

1 medium cucumber, thinly
sliced

¼ cup plain or tarragon-
flavored wine vinegar

1. Cut cauliflower and broccoli into bite-sized
pieces. Place in 2-quart microwave-safe
casserole. Add water. Cover with casserole lid.

2. MICROWAVE (high) 5–6 minutes or until tender-
crisp. Drain and cool slightly. Combine oil, salt,
oregano, pepper, and garlic. Add to vegetables;
mix lightly. Cover and refrigerate overnight.

3. Just before serving, add onions, radishes,
cucumber, and vinegar; toss lightly. Serve in
salad bowl or on salad greens.

A pretty chicken dish is the main attraction in this dinner. Rice completes the meal for a total of 435 calories.

MENU
CHICKEN A L'ORANGE
VEGETABLE-RICE PILAF

TIME GUIDE
About 1 hour ahead:
Prepare Vegetable-Rice Pilaf, steps 1 and 2.
Prepare Chicken a L'Orange, steps 1 and 2.
Complete rice, steps 3-5.
Complete chicken, step 3.

CHICKEN A L'ORANGE

About 4 servings, 255 calories each

This delicious family entree is special enough to serve to guests.

2 whole chicken breasts (about 2 pounds), halved and skinned

Paprika

¼ cup orange juice

2 tablespoons orange marmalade

¼ teaspoon salt

⅛ teaspoon pepper

1 medium carrot, shredded

2 green onions, sliced (including tops)

1 tablespoon sugar

2 teaspoons cornstarch

1. Arrange chicken breasts in 10- by 6-inch microwave-safe baking dish. Sprinkle with paprika. Combine juice, marmalade, salt, and pepper. Spoon over chicken. Top with carrot and onions. Cover with plastic wrap.

2. MICROWAVE (high) 12–14 minutes or until chicken is done. Drain juices into 2-cup microwave-safe measure. Mix in sugar and cornstarch.

3. MICROWAVE (high), uncovered, 1–1½ minutes or until sauce boils and thickens, stirring once. Serve sauce with chicken.

VEGETABLE-RICE PILAF

**About 4 servings,
180 calories each**

This colorful combination of vegetables and rice makes a good accompaniment for meat and poultry dishes.

½ **cup chopped celery**

2 **green onions, sliced (including tops)**

1 **tablespoon margarine**

1 **cup water**

½ **cup uncooked long-grain white rice**

2 **teaspoons instant chicken bouillon**

¼ **teaspoon salt**

⅛ **teaspoon dried rosemary leaves**

1 **cup frozen peas**

2 **tablespoons sliced almonds**

1. Combine celery, onions, and margarine in 1-quart microwave-safe casserole. Cover with casserole lid.

2. MICROWAVE (high) 3–3½ minutes or until vegetables are just about tender, stirring once.

3. Add water, rice, bouillon, salt, and rosemary to vegetables. Cover.

4. MICROWAVE (high) 5–6 minutes or until boiling. Then MICROWAVE (low—30%) 12–14 minutes or until rice is tender. Add frozen peas. Cover.

5. MICROWAVE (high) 2–3 minutes or until peas are heated through. Let stand 5 minutes. Fluff with fork. Sprinkle with almonds.

TIP

● To use full power instead of low power in step 4, MICROWAVE 3 minutes and let stand 4 minutes, twice.

Serve chicken thighs in grand style with this menu. The lite variation of a classic salad completes the 305-calorie meal. The stuffing mixture and salad (except for tossing) can be done a few hours ahead to ease the last-minute preparation.

MENU
CHICKEN WITH WALDORF STUFFING
LITE CAESAR SALAD

TIME GUIDE
About 45 minutes ahead:
Prepare Lite Caesar Salad, steps 1 and 2.
Prepare Chicken with Waldorf Stuffing.
Complete salad, step 3.

CHICKEN WITH WALDORF STUFFING

About 4 servings, 220 calories each

Apple and celery lighten and flavor the stuffing for this chicken dish.

1 *apple, cored and chopped*

1 *cup thinly sliced celery*

1 *tablespoon margarine*

2 *teaspoons instant chicken bouillon*

1½ *cups crushed herb-seasoned stuffing*

½ *cup water*

2 *tablespoons chopped nuts*

4 *chicken thighs (about 1½ pounds), skinned*

1 *tablespoon grated Parmesan cheese*

⅛ *teaspoon paprika*

Chopped fresh parsley

1. Combine apple, celery, margarine, and bouillon in 8- by 8-inch microwave-safe baking dish. Cover with plastic wrap.

2. MICROWAVE (high) 4–5 minutes or until tender. Add stuffing, water, and nuts; mix lightly. Arrange chicken on top of stuffing. Combine Parmesan cheese and paprika, and sprinkle on chicken. Cover with plastic wrap.

3. MICROWAVE (high) 9–10 minutes or until chicken is done, rotating dish once. Garnish with parsley.

TIP

• Other favorite chicken pieces can be substituted for thighs.

LITE CAESAR SALAD

**About 4 servings,
85 calories each**

Use the microwave to make your own bread cubes. The microwave also works well for preparing a quick-cooked egg for salads and sandwiches.

1 slice bread, cubed

1 egg

6 cups torn romaine lettuce

1 cup (4 ounces) sliced fresh mushrooms

4 tablespoons lite Italian dressing

2 tablespoons Parmesan cheese

1. MICROWAVE (high) bread cubes on uncovered microwave-safe plate 1½–2 minutes or until dry, stirring twice. Set aside. Place egg in microwave-safe custard cup; pierce yolk and cover with plastic wrap.

2. MICROWAVE (high) 25 seconds. Let stand 30 seconds. Then MICROWAVE (high) 30–45 seconds or until set. Cut into small pieces. Set aside.

3. Toss romaine, mushrooms, and Italian dressing. Add bread cubes, egg, and Parmesan cheese; mix lightly.

TIPS

• Bread cubes can be sprinkled lightly with garlic salt.

• Other favorite greens can be used in place of romaine.

This springlike menu is a delight to serve and will be enjoyed by family and guests alike. It is hard to believe food so good can add up to only 330 calories for the entire meal. For additional do-ahead preparation, cook the spaghetti (just rinse it and add seasonings when ready to heat) and have the chicken rolls ready to microwave.

MENU
SAVORY CHICKEN ROLLS
LITE SPAGHETTI PARMESAN
CARROT-ASPARAGUS DUO

TIME GUIDE
About 50 minutes ahead:
Prepare Lite Spaghetti Parmesan, steps 1 and 2.
Prepare Savory Chicken Rolls.
Prepare Carrot-Asparagus Duo.
Complete spaghetti, steps 3 and 4, increasing time to 2-4 minutes.
Reheat chicken rolls, if necessary.

SAVORY CHICKEN ROLLS
**4 rolls,
140 calories each**

Turkey ham and mushrooms are tucked inside chicken to give it a delicious flavor.

10 ounces skinned and boned chicken breast (2 whole breasts)

2 slices turkey ham sandwich meat, halved

½ cup (2 ounces) finely chopped fresh mushrooms

1 clove garlic, minced

½ tablespoon margarine

½ tablespoon dry bread crumbs

½ tablespoon grated Parmesan cheese

¼ teaspoon paprika

Salt to taste (optional)

1. Cut chicken breasts in half to form 4 pieces. Flatten each between sheets of plastic wrap to ¼-inch thickness. Top each with a piece of ham, 2 tablespoons of mushrooms, and a little garlic. Roll up, tucking in ends. Fasten with toothpick. Place in 8-inch microwave-safe pie plate. Set aside.

2. MICROWAVE (high) margarine in uncovered small glass dish 30–45 seconds or until melted. Brush chicken rolls with margarine. Combine bread crumbs, Parmesan cheese, and paprika. Sprinkle over rolls. If desired, sprinkle with salt. Cover with paper towel.

3. MICROWAVE (medium-high—70%) 6½–7½ minutes or until chicken is done.

TIP

• To use full power instead of medium-high power in step 3, reduce time to 5–6 minutes.

LITE SPAGHETTI PARMESAN

About 4 servings, 150 calories each

The new calorie-reduced pasta cooks nicely in the microwave. Here, we have added a lite glaze.

7 cups hot water

½ teaspoon salt

4 ounces calorie-reduced spaghetti

3 tablespoons evaporated skim milk

1 tablespoon margarine

2 tablespoons grated Parmesan cheese

1 tablespoon snipped fresh parsley

½ teaspoon seasoned salt

1. MICROWAVE (high) water and salt in uncovered 2-quart microwave-safe mixing bowl 7–8 minutes or until steaming hot. Add spaghetti.
2. MICROWAVE (high), uncovered, 14–15 minutes or until tender, stirring twice. Let stand 5 minutes. Drain.
3. Add milk, margarine, Parmesan cheese, parsley, and seasoned salt; mix lightly.
4. MICROWAVE (high), uncovered, 1–2 minutes or until heated through.

TIP

- Regular spaghetti can be used, but the calorie count will be higher. Reduce cooking time in step 2 to 6–7 minutes.

CARROT-ASPARAGUS DUO

About 4 servings, 40 calories each

A colorful combination of garden vegetables.

1 cup sliced carrots

2 tablespoons water

2 cups cut or snapped fresh asparagus

1 teaspoon cornstarch

½ teaspoon dried dill weed

¼ teaspoon garlic salt

1 teaspoon water

1. Combine carrots and water in 1-quart microwave-safe casserole. Cover with casserole lid.
2. MICROWAVE (high) 3 minutes. Add asparagus; cover.
3. MICROWAVE (high) 3½–4½ minutes or until just about tender. Combine cornstarch, dill, garlic salt, and water in small dish; blend well. Stir into vegetables.
4. MICROWAVE (high), uncovered, 30–60 seconds or until mixture boils and thickens, stirring once.

Plenty of vegetables and rice on the side help extend the protein in this menu, which totals 300 calories. Rice reheats nicely in the microwave, so it can be prepared ahead for reheating after preparing the Moo Goo Gai Pan.

MENU
MOO GOO GAI PAN
FLUFFY PARSLEYED RICE

TIME GUIDE
About 45 minutes ahead:
Prepare Fluffy Parsleyed Rice.
Prepare Moo Goo Gai Pan.

MOO GOO GAI PAN

**About 4 servings,
180 calories each**

A colorful and crunchy combination based on an Oriental classic. Chicken and lots of vegetables in a mild sauce make it familiar enough for family, yet tasty enough for company.

1 medium onion, cut into chunks

1 cup sliced celery

2 cups (8 ounces) small whole fresh mushrooms

¼ cup water

2 tablespoons dry sherry

6 ounces fresh pea pods (about 1½ cups)

1 tablespoon cornstarch

½ teaspoon grated fresh gingerroot

½ teaspoon salt

⅛ teaspoon pepper

2 cups cubed cooked chicken

1 8-ounce can sliced water chestnuts, drained

1. Combine onion, celery, mushrooms, water, and sherry in 2- to 2½-quart microwave-safe casserole. Cover with casserole lid.

2. MICROWAVE (high) 3 minutes. Mix in pea pods, cornstarch, gingerroot, salt, and pepper. Cover.

3. MICROWAVE (high) 2–3 minutes or until mixture boils and thickens. Add chicken and water chestnuts. Cover.

4. MICROWAVE (high) 2–3 minutes or until heated through.

TIP

- One 6-ounce package of frozen pea pods can be substituted for fresh.

FLUFFY PARSLEYED RICE

**About 6 servings,
120 calorie each**

Although cooking rice in the microwave will not save you much time, the results are great. No more sticky rice from overcooking.

1 **cup uncooked long-grain
  white rice**

1 **teaspoon salt**

1 **teaspoon margarine**

1¾ **cups water**

2 **tablespoons snipped fresh
  parsley**

1. Combine all ingredients except parsley in 1½-quart microwave-safe casserole. Cover with casserole lid.

2. MICROWAVE (high) 5–6 minutes or until mixture boils. Then MICROWAVE (low—30%) 12–14 minutes or until rice is tender. Let stand 5 minutes. Add parsley; fluff with fork.

TIP

- To use full power instead of the lower power in step 2, MICROWAVE 3 minutes and let stand 4 minutes, twice.

Here's another start-to-finish family meal that takes less than an hour to microwave. Since the gelatin salad requires refrigeration, be sure to start it the night before. Main dish and salad total only 280 calories.

MENU
COLORFUL MACARONI AND CHEESE
FRESH FRUIT GELATIN SALAD

TIME GUIDE
Several hours ahead or night before:
Prepare Fresh Fruit Gelatin Salad, steps 1–3.

About 45 minutes ahead:
Prepare Colorful Macaroni and Cheese.
Complete salad, step 4.

COLORFUL MACARONI AND CHEESE

About 4 servings, 215 calories each

Broccoli and carrots make a colorful addition to this family favorite.

6 cups hot water

1 teaspoon salt

1 cup rotini or regular macaroni

3 medium carrots, sliced

2 tablespoons chopped onion

2 tablespoons chopped celery

2 tablespoons water

2 cups broccoli pieces

⅓ cup skim milk

2 teaspoons cornstarch

¼ teaspoon salt

Dash pepper

4 ounces cubed processed cheese spread (about ¾ cup)

1. Combine 6 cups hot water, 1 teaspoon salt, and rotini in 2-quart microwave-safe mixing bowl.

2. MICROWAVE (high), uncovered, 12–14 minutes or until rotini is just about tender, stirring once. Let stand about 5 minutes. Drain and set aside.

3. Combine carrots, onion, celery, and 2 tablespoons water in 1-quart microwave-safe casserole. Cover with casserole lid.

4. MICROWAVE (high) 3 minutes. Stir in broccoli. Cover.

5. MICROWAVE (high) 2–3 minutes or until just about tender. Add milk and cornstarch; mix lightly. Add ¼ teaspoon salt, pepper, and cheese spread. Cover.

6. MICROWAVE (high), 3–4 minutes or until sauce boils and thickens slightly, stirring once. Add rotini; mix lightly.

TIP

• Other favorite vegetables can be substituted. Mixed vegetables, green beans, or peas would be good.

FRESH FRUIT GELATIN SALAD

**About 6 servings,
65 calories each**

Create your own gelatin salads using seasonal fresh fruit.

½ cup water

1 envelope unflavored gelatin

1 ripe banana

1½ cups fresh fruit (strawberries, raspberries, peaches, blueberries, melon)

1 tablespoon honey

2 teapoons lemon juice

½ teaspoon grated orange peel (optional)

2 tablespoons plain yogurt

1 tablespoon mayonnaise or salad dressing

1. Combine water and gelatin in 1-cup microwave-safe measure. Let stand 5 minutes to soften gelatin.

2. MICROWAVE (high), uncovered, 1–1½ minutes or until gelatin is dissolved. Set aside.

3. Process banana and other fruit in blender or food processor until smooth. Add honey, lemon juice, and orange peel. Process until smooth. Blend in warm gelatin mixture. Pour into 6 individual molds or a serving bowl. Refrigerate until set, about 4 hours.

4. Combine yogurt and mayonnaise. Serve salad on lettuce leaves, topped with yogurt mixture.

TIP

• Frozen fruit can be substituted for fresh; gelatin will set faster.

This 420-calorie menu is very homey yet refreshing with a bit of an Oriental flavor. Serve it often in summer and fall months when you want a change from normal fare.

MENU
CHICKEN AND RICE SOUP
SPINACH SALAD SUPREME

TIME GUIDE
At least 3 hours ahead:
Prepare Spinach Salad Supreme, step 1.
Prepare Chicken and Rice Soup, steps 1 and 2.

About 15 minutes ahead:
Complete soup, steps 3 and 4.
Complete salad, step 2.

CHICKEN AND RICE SOUP

**About 6 servings,
190 calories each**

Here is a quick family-type soup. While it cooks, you have ample time to prepare the salad.

**8–10 ounces chicken pieces
(wings, thighs, breasts,
etc.)**

2 carrots, sliced

1 medium onion, chopped

5 cups water

⅓ cup uncooked white rice

**1 tablespoon instant chicken
bouillon**

¾ teaspoon salt

⅛ teaspoon pepper

**⅛ teaspoon dried thyme
leaves or poultry
seasoning**

1½ cups fresh broccoli pieces

1. Combine all ingredients except broccoli in 3-quart microwave-safe casserole. Cover with casserole lid.

2. MICROWAVE (high) 23–25 minutes or until chicken is tender.

3. Remove chicken and allow to cool. Add broccoli to soup. Cover.

4. MICROWAVE (high) 5–6 minutes or until broccoli is tender. Bone chicken and cut into pieces; stir into soup.

TIP

• Cubed zucchini or chopped cabbage can be substituted for broccoli.

SPINACH SALAD SUPREME

**About 6 servings,
230 calories each**

*We figured these calories for a main dish meal; however, the servings could be smaller
for an accompaniment salad, with calories reduced accordingly.*

½ **cup chopped onion**

⅓ **cup cooking oil**

1 **3-ounce package Oriental-
flavored noodle soup mix
(Ramen)**

2 **tablespoons sugar**

2 **tablespoons vinegar**

½ **teaspoon salt**

¼ **teaspoon pepper**

4 **ounces tofu, drained, rinsed,
and cubed**

8 **cups torn spinach leaves**

2 **tablespoons sunflower seeds**

1. MICROWAVE (high) onion and oil in uncovered
   2-cup microwave-safe measure 2½–3 minutes or
   until onion is tender. Stir in flavor packet from
   soup mix (reserve noodles), sugar, vinegar, salt,
   and pepper; mix well. Add tofu. Cover and
   refrigerate at least 3 hours, allowing flavors to
   blend.

2. Place spinach in large serving bowl. Break
   uncooked noodles from mix into small pieces
   and mix well with spinach. Add dressing; toss
   lightly. Sprinkle with sunflower seeds.

TIP

• Tofu may be omitted; the calorie count will be lower.

Lasagna and French bread take on a new twist in this 380-calorie menu. It's a flavorful meal that's suitable for any time of the year. You'll be surprised at how quickly lasagna heats in its new shape! Much of the preparation can be done in advance, leaving just the final heating of the lasagna and bread for right before serving.

MENU
FLORENTINE LASAGNA ROLL-UPS
POPPY SEED BREAD

TIME GUIDE
About 45 minutes ahead:
Prepare Florentine Lasagna Roll-Ups, steps 1 and 2.
Prepare Poppy Seed Bread, steps 1 and 2.
Complete lasagna, steps 3–5.
Complete bread, step 3.

FLORENTINE LASAGNA ROLL-UPS

**4 servings,
275 calorie each**

Spinach makes these lasagna roll-ups so flavorful that no one will notice there's no meat.

- *4 lasagna noodles*
- *1 10-ounce package frozen chopped spinach*
- *1 cup low-fat cottage cheese*
- *1 egg, slightly beaten*
- *¼ teaspoon garlic powder*
- *¾ cup spaghetti sauce*
- *1 cup (4 ounces) shredded mozzarella cheese*

1. Cook noodles as directed on package. Drain and rinse in cold water. Set aside. Place spinach in 1-quart microwave-safe casserole. Cover with casserole lid.

2. MICROWAVE (high) 4–5 minutes or until thawed and heated, stirring once. Squeeze out excess liquid. Stir in cottage cheese, egg, and garlic powder.

3. Lay noodles on flat surface; divide spinach mixture evenly among noodles, spreading evenly. Roll up each with spinach mixture inside. Place roll-ups in 8- by 8-inch microwave-safe baking dish. Spoon spaghetti sauce over rolls. Cover with plastic wrap.

4. MICROWAVE (high) 4½–5½ minutes or until heated through (140°F), rotating once. Sprinkle with mozzarella cheese.

5. MICROWAVE (high), uncovered, 1–1½ minutes or until cheese melts.

POPPY SEED BREAD

**About 8 servings,
105 calories each**

Try this interesting twist to French bread.

*1 small loaf (8 ounces) French
bread*

2 tablespoons margarine

3 tablespoons chopped onion

2 teaspoons poppy seed

*2 tablespoons grated Parmesan
cheese*

1. Cut bread almost in half lengthwise and fold
   open; set aside.

2. MICROWAVE (high) margarine and onion in
   uncovered 2-cup microwave-safe measure 1½–2½
   minutes or until onion is tender. Stir in poppy
   seed. Brush mixture onto open sides of cut
   bread. Sprinkle with Parmesan cheese. Close
   bread; wrap in paper toweling.

3. MICROWAVE (high) 45–60 seconds or until
   bread just feels warm. Slice into 1½-inch pieces.

This menu is especially nice for spring since it includes new potatoes and asparagus—all for only 245 calories. It makes such a nice combination, you will want to substitute other seasonal vegetables or use frozen products for year 'round enjoyment.

MENU
FRENCH CHICKEN STRIPS
BUTTERED NEW POTATOES

TIME GUIDE
About 30 minutes ahead:
Prepare Buttered New Potatoes, steps 1 and 2.
Prepare French Chicken Strips.
Complete potatoes, steps 3 and 4.

FRENCH CHICKEN STRIPS

**About 4 servings,
150 calories each**

A spring delight . . . golden chicken strips with tender asparagus spears.

**10 ounces skinned and boned
  chicken breast**

1 tablespoon margarine

1 tablespoon dry bread crumbs

¼ teaspoon paprika

1 pound fresh asparagus

1 tablespoon fresh lemon juice

Dash ground nutmeg

1. Cut chicken into thin strips. Set aside. Place margarine in 8-inch round microwave-safe baking dish.

2. MICROWAVE (high), uncovered, 45–60 seconds or until margarine is melted. Add chicken pieces; mix lightly to coat with butter. Combine crumbs and paprika; sprinkle over chicken. Cover with paper towel.

3. MICROWAVE (high), 3–3½ minutes or until chicken is partially cooked. Carefully push chicken to center of dish.

4. Trim asparagus spears, breaking or cutting off tough ends of stalks. Place whole stalks on either side of chicken. Cover with plastic wrap.

5. MICROWAVE (high) 5–7 minutes or until asparagus is tender. Drizzle with lemon juice; sprinkle with nutmeg.

TIPS

● Broccoli spears can be substituted for asparagus.

● For larger quantities, increase the cooking time in proportion to the increase in quantity.

BUTTERED NEW POTATOES

**About 4 servings,
95 calories each**

Enjoy the flavor of these new potatoes with a lite butter glaze.

1½ **pounds (about 8–12 small)
new potatoes**

2 **tablespoons water**

1 **tablespoon butter or
margarine**

¼ **teaspoon dry mustard**

¼ **teaspoon salt**

⅛ **teaspoon lemon pepper**

1. Scrub potatoes and cut thin strip of peel from center of each potato. Place in 1-quart microwave-safe casserole. Add water and cover with casserole lid.

2. MICROWAVE (high) 7–8 minutes or until just about tender, rearranging once. Let stand, covered, 5 minutes. Drain.

3. Add butter, mustard, salt, and pepper. Cover.

4. MICROWAVE (high) 1–2 minutes or until butter is melted. Stir to coat potatoes.

CHAPTER
4
MINI-MEALS

Rather than devote a chapter of this book exclusively to meals to serve for lunch as we commonly know it, we developed fun, interesting menus that are appropriate for brunch, lunch, a lite supper, or an afternoon or late night snack. These mini-meals tie in with the concept that we are becoming a "grazing" society, consuming several smaller meals throughout the day, rather than eating the three "square" meals that were once the norm. This type of meal fits well with the busy on-the-go-lifestyle so many of us lead today.

We have included a few lite variations on the standard soup and sandwich theme. In addition, you'll discover creative recipes for main dish salads and omelets as well as sweet but nutritious dessert alternatives. Serve the menus as suggested, or mix and match, putting together other appealing combinations for your own mini-meals. When you want a lite but not empty-calorie snack, make just one item from a menu. A total calorie count is given for each menu, which includes the recipes given. These range from 180 to 320 calories for the menus included.

A plus for some of the recipes is that they make larger quantities that can be refrigerated or frozen and used as needed. You will find ideas like this for sandwiches, salads, and desserts to serve individually or in multiple servings.

Remember to use your microwave to simplify any mini-meal preparation. Heat soups, sandwiches, and frozen pizzas; melt cheese for snacks like nachos; and warm favorite beverages. Bars, cakes, and cookies are easily thawed in just a few seconds in the microwave. And you can heat some of last night's leftovers for a quick mini-meal to enjoy any time of the day or night.

So, when hunger strikes and you need a lite, tasty snack or meal, just turn to this chapter and prepare some fun creations for you and your family to enjoy.

A hot bowl of chili served with vegetable-topped pita bread makes a lite yet satisfying meal with only 300 calories. Either dish can be served alone or combined with other favorite lunch-type dishes.

MENU
CHILI
VEGGIE ROUNDS

TIME GUIDE
About 30 minutes ahead:
Prepare Chili.
Prepare Veggie Rounds.

CHILI

**About 4 servings,
190 calories each**

Always a family favorite.

½ **pound lean ground beef**

½ **cup chopped green pepper**

1 **tablespoon instant minced onion**

1 **16-ounce can whole tomatoes, undrained**

1 **cup drained, cooked kidney beans**

1–2 **teaspoons chili powder**

½ **teaspoon salt**

¼ **teaspoon paprika**

1. Combine ground beef, green pepper, and onion in 1½-quart microwave-safe casserole.
2. MICROWAVE (high), uncovered, 3–4 minutes or until meat is no longer pink, stirring once. Add tomatoes, beans, chili powder, salt, and paprika; mix well.
3. MICROWAVE (high), uncovered, 11–12 minutes or until hot and bubbly and flavors are blended, stirring once.

TIPS

- Use half of a 16-ounce can of beans or an 8-ounce can. Leftovers can be frozen for another use.
- Ground turkey can be substituted for beef.

VEGGIE ROUNDS

**4 sandwiches,
110 calories each**

Fresh garden vegetables are layered in these tasty open-faced sandwiches.

2 4-inch pita breads

1 tablespoon yogurt

1 tablespoon mayonnaise

¾ cup shredded zucchini

¼ cup shredded carrot

½ tomato, chopped

1 green onion, sliced

½ teaspoon salad seasoning

**¾ cup (3 ounces) shredded
Monterey Jack cheese**

1. Carefully slit open pita breads to make 4 rounds. Spread inner side of each round with a combination of yogurt and mayonnaise. Top each with equal amounts of zucchini, carrot, tomato, and onion. Sprinkle each with salad seasoning. Top with cheese.

2. Preheat browning dish by MICROWAVING (high) for about 6 minutes. Place rounds on hot dish.

3. MICROWAVE (high), uncovered, 1½–2 minutes or until cheese begins to melt.

TIPS

● Whole wheat or rye bread can be substituted for pita bread. When substituting bread slices, toast before using.

● When a browning dish is not available, place sandwiches on a paper plate and microwave as directed in step 3.

Single-serving cheesecakes complement a colorful pasta-vegetable salad in this 265-calorie meal. Enjoy the make-ahead convenience when your time will be at a premium.

MENU
TORTELLINI SALAD
INDIVIDUAL CHEESECAKES

TIME GUIDE
Day before or 3 hours ahead:
Prepare Tortellini Salad.
Prepare Individual Cheesecakes.

TORTELLINI SALAD

**About 4 servings,
185 calories each**

This pasta salad has a lite dressing and lots of fresh vegetables.

- *4 cups hot water*
- *½ teaspoon salt*
- *½ teaspoon cooking oil*
- *½ 7-ounce package dried tortellini with cheese filling*
- *4 ounces skinned and boned chicken breast*
- *1½ cups small broccoli pieces*
- *1½ cups small cauliflower pieces*
- *2 tablespoons olive or cooking oil*
- *2 tablespoons lemon juice*
- *2 tablespoons dry white wine*
- *½ teaspoon Worcestershire sauce*
- *¼ teaspoon dry mustard*
- *¼ teaspoon dried tarragon leaves*
- *¼ teaspoon salt*
- *1 clove garlic, minced*
- *2 green onions, sliced*
- *2 tablespoons diced red pepper*

1. Combine water, ½ teaspoon salt, ½ teaspoon oil, and tortellini in 2-quart microwave-safe casserole.
2. MICROWAVE (high), uncovered, 13–15 minutes or until pasta is tender, stirring once. Drain, rinse, and set aside.
3. Place chicken in 1½-quart shallow microwave-safe baking dish; cover with plastic wrap.
4. MICROWAVE (high), 2–2½ minutes or until just about tender. Add broccoli and cauliflower. Cover with plastic wrap.
5. MICROWAVE (high) 3–3½ minutes or until vegetables are tender-crisp. Uncover and set aside.
6. Combine drained tortellini and remaining ingredients in serving bowl. Add broccoli and cauliflower. Cut chicken into bite-sized pieces. Add to salad; mix lightly. Refrigerate until chilled.

TIPS

- Other favorite pastas such as macaroni or rigatoni can be substituted for tortellini.
- Chicken can be omitted. If desired, substitute favorite cooked meat or cheese.

INDIVIDUAL CHEESECAKES

**About 8 cheesecakes,
80 calories each**

Serve these low-cal mini-cheesecakes topped with fresh fruit slices.

¼ **cup skim milk**

½ **tablespoon unflavored gelatin**

1 **egg**

¼ **cup sugar**

1 **cup low-fat cottage cheese**

¼ **teaspoon vanilla**

8 **vanilla wafers**

Fresh fruit (optional)

1. Combine milk and gelatin in 1-cup microwave-safe measure. Beat in egg and sugar.

2. MICROWAVE (high), uncovered, 1½–2 minutes or until mixture is thickened and creamy, stirring once or twice. Beat until smooth.

3. Combine cottage cheese and vanilla in blender or food processor container. Process at medium speed until smooth. Blend in custard mixture. Line muffin pans with paper liners; place one vanilla wafer in bottom of each. Fill three-fourths full with cheesecake mixture. Refrigerate until set, about 2 hours. Top each with a slice of fresh fruit, if desired.

Taste the flavors of the Orient in this meal, which includes a main dish chicken salad served with coconut-topped orange slices. It is lite, colorful, and refreshing, with only about 220 calories per serving.

MENU
CHING CHANG SALAD
AMBROSIA ORANGES

TIME GUIDE
At least 1 hour ahead:
Prepare Ambrosia Oranges, steps 1 and 2.
Prepare Ching Chang Salad, steps 1-3.

About 30 minutes ahead:
Complete salad, steps 4-6.
Complete oranges, step 3.

CHING CHANG SALAD

**About 4 servings,
140 calories each**

This combination of Oriental vegetables and noodles is good served warm or chilled.

5 ounces skinned and boned chicken breast

¼ teaspoon chili powder

1 teaspoon grated fresh gingerroot

3 tablespoons soy sauce

2 medium carrots, shredded

4 cups hot water

3 ounces Oriental-style noodles

1½ cups fresh bean sprouts

1 cucumber, peeled and chopped

3 cups thinly sliced Chinese cabbage (Napa)

1. Place chicken breast in shallow microwave-safe baking dish. Sprinkle with chili powder and gingerroot. Add soy sauce. Cover with lid or plastic wrap.

2. MICROWAVE (high) 2–2½ minutes or until chicken is hot. Add carrots; cover.

3. MICROWAVE (high) 3–4 minutes or until chicken is done. Set aside.

4. MICROWAVE (high) water in 2-quart microwave-safe mixing bowl 8–9 minutes or until boiling. Add noodles and mix lightly with fork.

5. MICROWAVE (high), uncovered, 3–3½ minutes or until tender. Add bean sprouts and let stand about 30 seconds. Drain and rinse well in water.

6. Remove chicken and cut into bite-sized pieces. Add to noodles along with carrots and juices from dish; mix lightly. Mix in cucumber and cabbage. Serve immediately or chill.

TIPS

● Other favorite vegetables can be added or substituted.

● A dash of ground ginger can be substituted for gingerroot.

AMBROSIA ORANGES

**About 3 servings,
80 calories each**

Serve these for a quick salad, dessert, or snack. Keep extra coconut on hand to quickly dress up other fresh fruit.

¼ **cup flaked coconut**

½ **teaspoon water**

2 oranges

1. Combine coconut and water in microwave-safe custard cup; mix lightly.

2. MICROWAVE (high), uncovered, 2–3 minutes or until golden brown, stirring every 30 seconds. Cool slightly.

3. Peel oranges; slice horizontally into thin slices. Arrange on serving plate. Sprinkle with coconut.

Tomatoes filled with shrimp salad make a cool entree for warm summer days. Sweet Fruit-Nut Balls complete the 265-calorie meal.

MENU
SHRIMP SALAD IN TOMATO CUPS
FRUIT-NUT BALLS

TIME GUIDE
About 1 hour ahead or night before:
Prepare Shrimp Salad in Tomato Cups.
Prepare Fruit-Nut Balls.

SHRIMP SALAD IN TOMATO CUPS

**About 4 servings,
175 calories each**

This is a perfect entree for light luncheons.

4 medium tomatoes

2 green onions, sliced thin

¾ cup thinly sliced celery

¼ cup mayonnaise or salad dressing

¼ cup plain yogurt

½ teaspoon Beau Monde seasoning

Dash hot pepper sauce

1 6-ounce package frozen cooked shrimp, rinsed and drained

Chopped fresh parsley for garnish (optional)

1. Cut a thin slice from stem end of each tomato. Scoop out pulp with a spoon. Let tomato shells stand upside down on paper towels to drain.

2. Combine onions and celery in 2-cup microwave-safe measure.

3. MICROWAVE (high), uncovered, 1½–2 minutes or until vegetables are tender-crisp, stirring once; drain. Cool slightly. Combine mayonnaise, yogurt, Beau Monde, and hot pepper sauce. Mix lightly with shrimp and vegetables. Fill tomato shells with mixture; garnish with parsley. Refrigerate until served.

FRUIT-NUT BALLS

**About 30 balls,
45 calories each**

These chewy snacks can be microwaved right in the mixing bowl.

1 egg
⅓ cup sugar
½ cup flaked coconut
½ cup chopped dried apricots
½ cup chopped walnuts
¼ cup chopped dates
½ teaspoon vanilla
¼ teaspoon almond extract
½ cup crisp rice cereal

1. Beat egg slightly in 1-quart microwave-safe mixing bowl. Mix in sugar. Add coconut, apricots, walnuts, and dates; stir to combine.

2. MICROWAVE (high), uncovered, 3½–4 minutes or until mixture thickens enough to hold its shape, stirring once or twice. Mix in vanilla and almond extract. Cool completely. Stir in cereal.

3. Form mixture into 1-inch balls. Store in covered container. Allow 2 balls per serving.

TIP

● Mixture is sticky. Butter hands or rinse often with water for ease in forming balls.

This easy-to-make menu is perfect for lunch or a light supper. It's table-ready in about 15 minutes and has only 225 calories per serving.

MENU
TERRIFIC TURKEY TOSTADAS
APPLE S'MORES

TIME GUIDE
About 15 minutes ahead:
Prepare Terrific Turkey Tostadas, steps 1–3.
Prepare Apple S'mores, step 1.

About 5 minutes ahead:
Complete tostadas, steps 4 and 5.
Complete s'mores, step 2.

TERRIFIC TURKEY TOSTADAS

About 5 servings, 190 calories each

Ground turkey has fewer calories than beef. When served in a tomato sauce, the flavor is so similar that no one will know the difference.

½ pound ground turkey

1 8-ounce can tomato sauce

½ teaspoon chili powder

½ teaspoon ground cumin

½ teaspoon salt

⅛ teaspoon garlic powder

5 tostada shells

1 cup shredded lettuce

½ tomato, chopped

½ cup (2 ounces) shredded cheddar cheese

Bottled taco sauce (optional)

1. Crumble ground turkey into 1-quart microwave-safe casserole.

2. MICROWAVE (high), uncovered, 2½–3½ minutes or until no longer pink. Stir to break turkey into pieces. Stir in tomato sauce, chili powder, cumin, salt, and garlic powder.

3. MICROWAVE (high), uncovered, 5–6 minutes or until mixture boils, stirring once or twice. Then MICROWAVE (medium—50%) 5–7 minutes or until flavors are blended. Set aside. Unwrap tostada shells; wrap in paper towels.

4. MICROWAVE (high) 30–45 seconds or until warm.

5. Top each tostada with scant ⅓ cup turkey mixture. Sprinkle on lettuce, tomato, and cheese. Serve with taco sauce.

APPLE S'MORES

Popular flavors are sandwiched between apple slices.

1 apple
16 miniature marshmallows
16 semisweet chocolate pieces

1. Remove stem and blossom end of apple. Slice horizontally into 8 slices. Remove any seeds. Place 4 slices on microwave-safe serving plate. Top each slice with 4 marshmallows and 4 chocolate pieces.

2. MICROWAVE (high), uncovered, 20–30 seconds or until marshmallows are soft and chocolate is glossy. Top each with remaining apple slices. Serve warm.

For just 230 calories, you can enjoy a vegetable-topped omelet served with a blend of seasonal fresh fruit. It is light yet satisfying.

MENU
VEGETARIAN OMELET
SUMMERTIME FRUIT CUP

TIME GUIDE
About 30 minutes ahead:
Prepare Summertime Fruit Cup.
Prepare Vegetarian Omelet.

VEGETARIAN OMELET

**About 4 servings,
120 calories each**

A variety of vegetables fill this omelet.

1 cup (4 ounces) sliced fresh mushrooms

1 cup torn fresh spinach leaves

1 cup fresh bean sprouts

1 clove garlic, minced

1 tablespoon margarine

4 eggs

⅛ teaspoon salt

Soy sauce

1. Combine mushrooms, spinach, sprouts, garlic, and margarine in 3-cup microwave-safe casserole. Cover with casserole lid.

2. MICROWAVE (high) 3–3½ minutes or until vegetables are tender-crisp. Beat eggs until blended; mix in salt. Pour over vegetables. Cover.

3. MICROWAVE (high) 1 minute. Stir lightly. Cover.

4. MICROWAVE (high) 30–60 seconds or until eggs are just about set. Let stand a few minutes. Loosen sides and invert onto serving plate. Cut into wedges and serve with a little soy sauce.

SUMMERTIME FRUIT CUP

**About 4 servings,
110 calories each**

A lite orange sauce flavors this delightful combination of fresh fruit. It's sure to be a family favorite.

3 tablespoons sugar

1 teaspoon cornstarch

2 tablespoons frozen orange
   juice concentrate

¼ cup water

1 cup melon balls

1 cup sliced fresh peaches

1 cup sliced fresh strawberries

1 cup grapes

1. Combine sugar, cornstarch, orange juice concentrate, and water in 2-cup microwave-safe measure.

2. MICROWAVE (high), uncovered, 2–3 minutes or until mixture boils and thickens, stirring once. Set aside to cool. Combine melon, peaches, strawberries, and grapes in 1-quart bowl. Pour sauce over; mix well. Serve immediately or chill.

Enjoy homemade granola bars and a fruity low-calorie milk shake for a refreshing 200-calorie midday pick-me-up. You will find them so good that you will want to serve them alone or with other combinations, too.

MENU
GRANOLA BARS
LO-CAL STRAWBERRY MILK SHAKE

TIME GUIDE
Several hours ahead:
Prepare Granola Bars.

About 10 minutes ahead:
Prepare Lo-Cal Strawberry Milk Shake.

GRANOLA BARS

**About 24 bars,
45 calories each**

You can make homemade granola bars easily in your microwave.

2 tablespoons brown sugar

2 tablespoons light corn syrup

2 tablespoons margarine

2 tablespoons peanut butter

¼ teaspoon vanilla

1¼ cups granola cereal (crush if chunky)

⅔ cup crisp rice cereal

1. Combine brown sugar, corn syrup, and margarine in 2-quart microwave-safe mixing bowl.

2. MICROWAVE (high), uncovered, 1–1½ minutes or until mixture boils, stirring once. Then MICROWAVE (high) 30 seconds longer.

3. Stir in peanut butter and vanilla. Mix in granola and rice cereal until evenly coated. Turn onto a sheet of waxed paper. Press with fingers or fork, forming a square ½ inch thick. Let stand several hours or until cool and set. Cut into bars.

TIP

● Peanut butter can be omitted. Add ¼ cup raisins or chocolate chips, if desired.

LO-CAL STRAWBERRY MILK SHAKE

**About 4 servings,
155 calories each**

Yogurt makes this shake a smooth and refreshing summer drink.

¼ *cup skim milk*

1 *teaspoon unflavored gelatin*

1 *cup (8 ounces) vanilla yogurt*

¾ *cup skim milk*

1 *banana*

½ *cup frozen strawberries*

1 *teaspoon vanilla*

2 *tablespoons honey*

10 *ice cubes*

1. Combine ¼ cup skim milk and gelatin in 1-cup microwave-safe measure.

2. MICROWAVE (high), uncovered, 45–60 seconds or until gelatin is dissolved. Combine remaining ingredients except ice in blender container; process until smooth. Blend in gelatin mixture. Add ice cubes, one at a time, processing until smooth. Pour into glasses and serve.

TIP

● Fresh strawberries can be substituted for frozen.

A steaming bowl of chowder and a warm dish of fruit crisp make a winning combination for cool days. Both dishes can be ready in about 30 minutes, and they total only 300 calories.

MENU
VEGETABLE-CLAM CHOWDER
PEAR CRISP

TIME GUIDE
About 30 minutes ahead:
Prepare Pear Crisp.
Prepare Vegetable-Clam Chowder.

VEGETABLE-CLAM CHOWDER

**About 4 servings,
140 calories each**

A colorful assortment of vegetables give this chowder extra flavor.

*2 medium carrots, sliced
(about 1 cup)*

1 medium onion, chopped

*1 medium zucchini, sliced
(about 1½ cups)*

1 cup chopped celery

*1 6½-ounce can minced clams,
undrained*

2½ cups skim milk

3 tablespoons flour

*1 teaspoon instant chicken
bouillon*

½ teaspoon garlic salt

⅛ teaspoon pepper

1. Combine carrots, onion, zucchini, celery, and liquid from clams in 2-quart microwave-safe casserole. Cover with casserole lid.

2. MICROWAVE (high) 10–12 minutes or until vegetables are tender, stirring once or twice. Add milk, flour, bouillon, garlic salt, and pepper to vegetables; mix until smooth.

3. MICROWAVE (high), uncovered, 5–6 minutes or until mixture boils and thickens, stirring twice. Stir in clams.

PEAR CRISP

**About 4 servings,
160 calories each**

Use fresh pears or other favorite seasonal fruit for this easy crisp.

**2 ripe pears, peeled, cored, and
   sliced (about 2 cups)**

2 tablespoons margarine

½ cup rolled oats

1 tablespoon flour

1 tablespoon brown sugar

½ teaspoon ground cinnamon

1. Place pear slices in 20-ounce microwave-safe casserole. Set aside.

2. MICROWAVE (high) margarine in small uncovered microwave-safe dish 30–45 seconds or until softened. Mix in rolled oats, flour, brown sugar, and cinnamon. Spoon evenly over pears.

3. MICROWAVE (high), uncovered, 4½–5½ minutes or until pears are tender. Serve warm or chilled.

TIP

● Other favorite fruits such as apples, peaches, rhubarb, or berries can be substituted for pears. Calories will vary accordingly.

Frozen individual fruit salads are made ahead and can be partially thawed while the omelet cooks. Enjoy this quick 295-calorie meal for brunch, lunch, or supper.

MENU
ASPARAGUS OMELET
FROZEN FRUIT DELITES

TIME GUIDE
Day before or at least 4 hours ahead:
Prepare Frozen Fruit Delites.

About 15 minutes ahead:
Remove desired number of Frozen Fruit Delites from freezer.
Prepare Asparagus Omelet.

ASPARAGUS OMELET

**About 2 servings,
195 calories each**

Vegetables make attractive and tasty fillings for omelets.

4 ounces fresh asparagus

3 eggs

¼ cup low-fat cottage cheese

½ teaspoon snipped chives

⅛ teaspoon dried thyme leaves

⅛ teaspoon salt

2 tablespoons shredded cheddar cheese

1. Break off tough ends of asparagus and discard. Wash asparagus well. Wrap in plastic wrap. Place on microwave-safe plate.

2. MICROWAVE (high) 2–3 minutes or until just about tender. Set aside.

3. Beat together eggs, cottage cheese, chives, thyme, and salt. Spray 9-inch microwave-safe pie plate with nonstick coating. Pour in egg mixture. Cover with plastic wrap.

4. MICROWAVE (high) 1 minute. Carefully move cooked portions to center. Cover.

5. MICROWAVE (high) 1–2½ minutes or until just about set. Arrange asparagus on half of omelet; sprinkle with cheddar cheese. Fold over other portion of omelet and slide onto serving plate. If necessary, microwave a few seconds longer to finish cooking egg.

TIP

- Elevating the pie plate on an inverted saucer will improve the cooking of the eggs in some ovens.

FROZEN FRUIT DELITES

**About 12 servings,
100 calories each**

Here's a delightful fruit combination to include in any meal. It's great to have in the freezer, especially during the warm summer months.

½ *cup water*

¼ *cup sugar*

1 *10-ounce package frozen sweetened strawberries*

1 *8-ounce can crushed pineapple in fruit juice, drained*

1 *8-ounce can apricots, drained and quartered*

2 *bananas, sliced*

½ *cup fresh or frozen blueberries*

1. Combine water and sugar in 2-cup microwave-safe measure; mix well.

2. MICROWAVE (high), uncovered, 1½–2½ minutes or until mixture boils; stir well. Then MICROWAVE (high) 1 minute longer; set aside.

3. MICROWAVE (high) strawberries in package 1½–2 minutes or until partially thawed. Combine strawberries, pineapple, apricots, bananas, and blueberries in 2-quart bowl. Add syrup; mix well. Spoon fruit mixture into about 12 paper-lined muffin cups. Freeze until firm, about 3 hours.

4. To serve, remove papers and let stand about 15 minutes to thaw partially. (Store leftovers in plastic bag in freezer.)

TIP

- Mixture can also be spooned into small paper cups. Insert wooden spoon in each when almost frozen to make fruitsicles.

Granola-topped yogurt teams up with a meat and vegetable salad for this cool, easy meal of just 305 calories. Much of the preparation is done well in advance.

MENU
ASPARAGUS AND BEEF VINAIGRETTE
YOGURT AND GRANOLA

TIME GUIDE
Several hours ahead:
Prepare Asparagus and Beef Vinaigrette, steps 1 and 2.
Prepare Yogurt and Granola, steps 1–3.

About 10 minutes ahead:
Complete salad, step 3.
Complete yogurt-granola, step 4.

ASPARAGUS AND BEEF VINAIGRETTE

About 4 servings, 185 calories each

A lite vinaigrette dressing tops fresh asparagus, sliced beef, and tomatoes in this bright and tasty salad. Serve with hard rolls for an easy meal.

1 pound fresh asparagus, cut into 1-inch pieces

2 tablespoons water

3 tablespoons cooking oil

3 tablespoons wine vinegar

1 clove garlic, minced

¼ teaspoon salt

1 cup sliced cooked beef

1 cup (4 ounces) sliced fresh mushrooms

10 cherry tomatoes, halved

1 tablespoon grated Parmesan cheese

1. Combine asparagus and water in 1½-quart microwave-safe casserole. Cover with casserole lid.

2. MICROWAVE (high) 5½–6½ minutes or until tender, stirring once; drain. Add oil, vinegar, garlic, salt, beef, and mushrooms; mix lightly. Cover and refrigerate until well chilled.

3. Just before serving, mix in tomatoes. Sprinkle with Parmesan cheese.

TIPS

- Sliced cooked chicken can be substituted for beef. Or omit the meat and serve as a salad or vegetable.

- Frozen cut asparagus can be substituted for fresh. Use 2 packages and MICROWAVE 8–10 minutes.

YOGURT AND GRANOLA

**About 3 cups,
20 calories/tablespoon granola,
plus 100 calories/½ cup yogurt**

Make your own granola easily in the microwave. This recipe is lightly sweetened with honey.

2 cups old-fashioned rolled oats

2 tablespoons sunflower seeds

2 tablespoons wheat germ

**2 tablespoons flaked coconut or
soy nut pieces**

Dash ground cinnamon

2 tablespoons cooking oil

2 tablespoons honey

½ teaspoon vanilla

Favorite fruit-flavored yogurt

1. Combine rolled oats, sunflower seeds, wheat germ, coconut, and cinnamon in 2-quart microwave-safe mixing bowl; mix lightly. Combine oil and honey in 1-cup microwave-safe measure.

2. MICROWAVE (high), uncovered, 20–30 seconds or until boiling. Blend in vanilla. Pour over rolled oats mixture; mix lightly.

3. MICROWAVE (high), uncovered, 6–8 minutes or until golden brown, stirring several times during last half of cooking time. Cool.

4. To serve, top ½ cup favorite fruit-flavored yogurt with 1 tablespoon granola.

TIPS

- Quick-cooking rolled oats can be used; texture will be a little finer.

- Other favorite nuts and seeds can be substituted or added. Calories will vary accordingly.

The classic Reuben sandwich takes on a new shape when served in pita bread. A light sauce for dipping your favorite fruit or cake squares rounds out the menu. When 1 tablespoon sauce is served with 1 cup strawberries, you have a menu of about 180 calories.

MENU
MINI REUBEN PITAS
FRESH FRUIT WITH LITE DESSERT SAUCE

TIME GUIDE
Day before or several hours ahead:
Prepare Lite Dessert Sauce.

About 10 minutes ahead:
Prepare Mini Reuben Pitas.

MINI REUBEN PITAS

**8 sandwiches,
110 calories each**

Have this corned beef mixture on hand and make sandwiches as you need them.

**4 whole wheat mini (4-inch) pita
breads**

3 ounces corned beef, chopped

**½ cup (2 ounces) shredded Swiss
cheese**

½ cup drained sauerkraut

1 tablespoon plain yogurt

**1 tablespoon Thousand Island
salad dressing**

Dash caraway seed (optional)

1. Cut pita breads in half to form semicircular pockets.

2. Combine corned beef, cheese, sauerkraut, yogurt, dressing, and caraway seed; mix lightly. Place a rounded spoonful of mixture into each pocket. Arrange on microwave-safe serving plate.

3. MICROWAVE (high), uncovered, 1½–2 minutes or until cheese starts to melt, rotating plate once.

TIPS

● To heat one sandwich, MICROWAVE 10–15 seconds.

● Filling will keep 3–4 days in refrigerator.

LITE DESSERT SAUCE

**About ¾ cup,
20 calories/tablespoon**

This lite cream cheese custard makes a delicious dipping sauce for fresh fruit or cake.

3 ounces Neufchâtel cheese

⅓ cup skim milk

2 tablespoons sugar

1 egg, slightly beaten

¼ teaspoon vanilla

1. MICROWAVE (high) Neufchâtel cheese in uncovered 2-cup microwave-safe measure 20–30 seconds or until softened. Blend in skim milk, sugar, and egg until smooth.

2. MICROWAVE (high), uncovered, 2–2½ minutes or until slightly thickened, stirring once or twice. Stir in vanilla. Cover and refrigerate at least 2 hours.

TIP

• Serve any leftover sauce over cake, fruit, or ice cream.

Lightly glazed fresh fruit accompanies an interesting tarragon-flavored chicken salad. Family or guests are sure to enjoy this 320-calorie meal. Since much of the preparation is done in advance, it is as easy to serve as it is attractive.

MENU
TARRAGON CHICKEN
GLAZED FRESH FRUIT

TIME GUIDE
Several hours ahead:
Prepare Tarragon Chicken, steps 1-3.
Prepare Glazed Fresh Fruit, steps 1 and 2.

About 30 minutes ahead:
Complete chicken, step 4.
Complete glazed fruit, step 3.

TARRAGON CHICKEN

**About 4 servings,
250 calories each**

This appealing salad plate includes lettuce, tomato, chicken strips, and sunflower seeds. It's topped with a tarragon-flavored vinaigrette dressing.

Dressing

¼ cup olive or cooking oil

3 tablespoons red wine vinegar

1 tablespoon Dijon mustard

1 teaspoon dried tarragon leaves

1 clove garlic, minced

¼ teaspoon salt

⅛ teaspoon pepper

Salad

6 ounces skinned and boned chicken breast

3 cups torn lettuce

1 medium tomato, chopped

2 tablespoons sunflower seeds

1 green onion, sliced (including top)

1. Combine dressing ingredients in small jar; cover. Shake until well blended; set aside.

2. Place chicken in 1½-quart shallow microwave-safe baking dish; cover with plastic wrap.

3. MICROWAVE (high) 3½–4½ minutes or until done, rotating dish once. Cool; cut into ½-inch strips.

4. Arrange lettuce on large serving plate or 4 individual plates. Top with tomato, chicken, sunflower seeds, and green onion. Drizzle dressing over salad.

GLAZED FRESH FRUIT

**About 4 servings,
70 calories each**

Serve this attractive fruit plate as an entree or accompaniment.

1 8½-ounce can lite sliced pears

Water

1 teaspoon cornstarch

1 small cantaloupe, peeled and
    seeded

1 kiwifruit, peeled and sliced
    thin

½ cup blueberries

1. Drain juice from pears into 2-cup microwave-safe measure. Add enough water to make ½ cup liquid. Set pears aside. Stir cornstarch into pear juice; blend until smooth.

2. MICROWAVE (high), uncovered, 1½–2 minutes or until sauce boils and thickens, stirring once. Set aside.

3. Cut cantaloupe into thin wedges; arrange on plate. Top with pears, kiwifruit, and blueberries. Drizzle glaze over fruit.

Pizzas with a salad topping and carrot bars make for a healthful, balanced 280-calorie meal. Both can be prepared in advance and then enjoyed at your convenience.

MENU
SALAD PIZZAS
CARROT BARS

TIME GUIDE
Several hours ahead:
Prepare Carrot Bars.

About 20 minutes ahead:
Prepare Salad Pizzas.

SALAD PIZZAS

**4 pizzas,
215 calories each**

Pita bread is the base for this "cool" version of pizza. Top it with your favorite combination of vegetables and meat.

1 cup sliced cauliflower

1 cup sliced broccoli

1 tablespoon water

2 6-inch pita breads

3 ounces Neufchâtel cheese

⅓ cup plain yogurt

½ teaspoon onion salt

½ teaspoon dill weed

1 tomato, quartered

1½ ounces sliced pepperoni (about 16 slices)

¼ cup sliced ripe olives

2 tablespoons grated Parmesan cheese

1. Combine cauliflower, broccoli, and water in 1-quart microwave-safe casserole. Cover with casserole lid.

2. MICROWAVE (high) 2–2½ minutes or until tender-crisp. Drain and cool.

3. Carefully slit open pita breads to make 4 rounds; place inner side up on a serving plate. Set aside. Place Neufchâtel cheese in small microwave-safe bowl.

4. MICROWAVE (high), uncovered, 30–45 seconds or until softened. Stir in yogurt, onion salt, and dill weed. Divide mixture evenly among pita bread rounds; spread to cover bread.

5. Cut each tomato quarter into 4 thin slices. Arrange 4 on each pocket bread round. Top each with one-quarter of cauliflower, broccoli, pepperoni, olives, and cheese. Serve immediately or refrigerate until served.

TIPS

- Other toppings might include sliced mushrooms, cucumber, radishes, green pepper, green olives, alfalfa sprouts, grated carrot, or other grated cheese and meat.

- Flour tortillas can be substituted for pita bread.

CARROT BARS

**About 20 bars,
65 calories each**

A jar of baby food makes this bar recipe quick and easy.

¼ cup margarine

½ cup sugar

1 egg

1 4½-ounce jar carrot baby food

¾ cup unsifted all-purpose flour

½ teaspoon soda

¼ teaspoon ground cinnamon

⅛ teaspoon ground nutmeg

⅛ teaspoon ground cloves

¼ cup flaked coconut

Powdered sugar

1. MICROWAVE (high) margarine in microwave-safe mixing bowl 15–30 seconds or until softened. Blend in sugar; beat in egg and baby food. Stir in remaining ingredients except coconut and powdered sugar; beat until smooth. Stir in coconut.

2. Pour into 8- by 8-inch microwave-safe baking dish, greased on bottom only. Cover with plastic wrap.

3. MICROWAVE (high) 4–5 minutes or until no longer doughy, rotating dish twice. Cool. Sprinkle with powdered sugar. Cut into bars.

TIPS

- If desired, use part whole wheat flour.

- Elevating the baking dish on an inverted saucer will help cook the bottom of the bars in some ovens.

- Banana baby food can be substituted for carrot.

CHAPTER
5
MEALS FOR ONE OR TWO

Cooking for one or two is a challenge, and at times it may just seem easier to stop at your favorite fast-food restaurant. But that kind of diet gets old in a hurry, puts a strain on the budget, and can shortchange you nutritionally. Rather, team your microwave and the menus in this chapter for tasty, economical, and healthful meals at home with little effort.

When cooking for one or two, you'll find your microwave indispensable. Cooking small amounts of food is what the microwave oven does best. But, while portions are quick to heat, they are also quick to overcook. You need to pay close attention, at least initially, and may even want to switch to a lower power setting with some foods. Leftovers or "planned overs" can be refrigerated or frozen and reheated easily.

Sometimes ingredients can be a problem when cooking for one or two since many food items are packaged in larger sizes. You can alleviate some of this problem by packaging in smaller amounts—¼- to ⅓-pound units—and freezing. Buy frozen vegetables in the "pourable" bags so you can use just the amount needed. Or wrap the part of a vegetable or ground beef block you want to keep frozen in foil and microwave to thaw the unwrapped portion. If you have extras of a canned item, for example, freeze it and microwave later to thaw. Make up your own seasoning and coating mixes to have on hand, such as taco seasoning or crumb coating mix for chicken or fish.

Having the right cooking utensils also helps ease the task of small-quantity cooking. There are several smaller-size microwave-safe dishes on the market. For example, several manufacturers make 6-ounce custard cups and 10- and 20-ounce casseroles. One- and 2-cup measures are useful not only for measuring, but also for heating soup, sauces, puddings, and small amounts of vegetables. Some lids from 1- and 2-quart casseroles can double as small pie plates when turned upside down. You'll be pleased to discover that many of the recipes in this book are cooked and served in the same dish.

There are a wide variety of dishes in this chapter. Most are geared to twosomes. If you are cooking for just one, refrigerate or freeze the extra portions for another meal. Or, if you're cooking for three or four and these recipes are appealing, most can be doubled. Also, check the chapter on "Freezer Meals" if you like the convenience of having single-serving quantities ready in the freezer. Many of those recipes include "Tips" for heating single servings.

Cooking for one or two can be fun and easy with delicious end results. Try some of the ideas in this chapter and see how much more interesting both cooking and eating can be.

Eggs with taco fixings give this colorful dish a south-of-the-border flair. At only 365 calories, it is perfect for a brunch or evening meal. Besides being colorful, tasty, and low in calories, it takes less than 20 minutes to prepare!

MENU
EGGS MEXICANA
ASPARAGUS AND CARROTS
AMBROSIA CUPS

TIME GUIDE
About 20 minutes ahead:
Prepare Asparagus and Carrots, steps 1 and 2.
Prepare Ambrosia Cups.
Prepare Eggs Mexicana, steps 1 and 2.
Complete asparagus, step 3.
Complete eggs, step 3.

EGGS MEXICANA

**About 2 servings,
215 calories each**

Mexican seasonings and taco fixings spice up this egg dish.

3 eggs

3 tablespoons water

Dash chili powder

Dash dried oregano leaves

Dash salt

¼ cup chunky taco sauce

¼ cup shredded cheddar cheese

Shredded lettuce (optional)

1. Beat together eggs, water, chili powder, oregano, and salt in 7-inch microwave-safe pie plate or shallow casserole.
2. MICROWAVE (high), uncovered, 2½–3 minutes or until eggs are almost set, stirring once during last half of cooking time. Spoon taco sauce over eggs; top with cheese.
3. MICROWAVE (high), uncovered, 1–2 minutes or until cheese is melted. Garnish with lettuce.

TIP

- The lids of some casseroles make good 7-inch pie plates when inverted. Otherwise, use a casserole of about that size.

ASPARAGUS AND CARROTS

**About 2 servings,
80 calories each**

Tarragon-glazed asparagus and carrots make a colorful vegetable side dish for many meals.

2 **carrots, peeled and cut into ½-inch slices (about ½ cup)**

2 **tablespoons water**

½ **pound fresh asparagus, cut into 1-inch pieces**

1 **tablespoon margarine**

¼ **teaspoon dried tarragon leaves**

1. Combine carrots and water in 3-cup microwave-safe casserole. Cover with casserole lid.

2. MICROWAVE (high) 2½–3 minutes or until carrots are tender-crisp. Add asparagus. Cover.

3. MICROWAVE (high) 3–3½ minutes or until asparagus is tender, stirring once. Drain. Add margarine and tarragon; mix lightly.

AMBROSIA CUPS

**About 2 servings,
70 calories each**

This refreshing fruit combination goes nicely with the spicy flavor of the Eggs Mexicana. It is also delicious served as a light snack.

1 **8-ounce can pineapple tidbits in fruit juice**

1 **teaspoon cornstarch**

½ **tablespoon sugar**

5 **maraschino cherries, halved**

½ **tablespoon flaked coconut**

1. Drain juice from pineapple into 2-cup microwave-safe measure. Stir in cornstarch and sugar.

2. MICROWAVE (high), uncovered, 1½–2 minutes or until mixture boils and thickens, stirring once. Stir in pineapple and cherries. Divide between 2 serving dishes. Sprinkle with coconut. Serve warm or cold.

TIP

- Other favorite fruit can be substituted for pineapple. Fresh strawberries or raspberries can be substituted for maraschino cherries. Use about ¼ cup.

This 440-calorie meal makes use of some convenience foods to keep the preparation simple. The total preparation takes about 30 minutes when everything is prepared in the microwave. To shorten this time, cook the pasta conventionally on a surface unit while preparing the vegetable sauce in the microwave.

MENU
FETTUCCINI WITH VEGETABLES
QUICK GARLIC ROLLS

TIME GUIDE
About 30 minutes ahead:
Prepare Fettuccini with Vegetables.
Prepare Quick Garlic Rolls.

FETTUCCINI WITH VEGETABLES

About 2 servings, 345 calories each

Pasta and a frozen vegetable blend are combined in a light sauce for this convenient meatless main dish.

4 cups hot water

½ teaspoon salt

4 ounces fettuccini

1½ cups frozen vegetable combination (broccoli, cauliflower, and carrots)

1 tablespoon margarine

½ cup skim milk

2 tablespoons or more grated Parmesan cheese

¼ teaspoon salt

¼ teaspoon dried basil leaves

1. MICROWAVE (high) water and salt in uncovered 2-quart microwave-safe mixing bowl 5–6 minutes or until steaming hot. Add fettuccini to water.

2. MICROWAVE (high), uncovered, 6–7 minutes or until just about tender, stirring once or twice. Let stand 5 minutes. Drain and rinse in cold water.

3. MICROWAVE (high) vegetables in uncovered 2-cup microwave-safe measure 2–2½ minutes or until thawed. Add margarine, milk, 2 tablespoons Parmesan cheese, salt, basil, and vegetables to fettuccini; toss lightly.

4. MICROWAVE (high), uncovered, 3½–4 minutes or until heated through, stirring once. If desired, serve with additional Parmesan cheese.

TIPS

- Lite spaghetti can be substituted for fettuccini. Increase cooking time to that indicated on package. Calories will be slightly lower.

- Other vegetable combinations can be used. Or make up your own combination of seasonal fresh vegetables.

- Cubed, cooked chicken or cooked shrimp can be added with seasonings.

QUICK GARLIC ROLLS

4 rolls,
95 calories each

Dress up bakery rolls with this easy filling. For larger quantities, just increase the ingredients and time proportionately.

4 bakery rolls

1 tablespoon margarine

Dash garlic salt

1 tablespoon grated Parmesan cheese

¼ teaspoon snipped chives

1. Cut rolls in half. Place on microwave-safe plate. Set aside.

2. MICROWAVE (high) margarine in small uncovered microwave-safe dish 15–20 seconds or until softened. Stir in remaining ingredients. Spread mixture on cut side of each bottom half of roll. Top with remaining roll half.

3. MICROWAVE (high), uncovered, 20–30 seconds or until rolls feel warm.

Zucchini is included as part of this small-sized lasagna recipe. Served with a vegetable, it's an easy meal for about 380 calories. When preparation time is limited at mealtime, assemble the lasagna early in the day or the night before. Then it takes just 15 minutes to heat.

MENU
TWOSOME LASAGNA
QUICK CREAMY BEANS

TIME GUIDE
About 30 minutes ahead:
Prepare Twosome Lasagna.
Prepare Quick Creamy Beans.

TWOSOME LASAGNA

**About 2 servings,
285 calories each**

This meatless lasagna tastes so good that you will want to make it often.

2 lasagna noodles

1 small zucchini, sliced

⅔ cup low-fat cottage cheese

¼ cup shredded mozzarella cheese

1 egg

½ teaspoon Italian seasoning

⅓ cup tomato sauce

1 tablespoon grated Parmesan cheese

1. Cook noodles as directed on package. Drain and rinse in cold water. Cut each noodle in half crosswise; set aside. Place zucchini in 2-cup microwave-safe measure. Cover with plastic wrap.

2. MICROWAVE (high) 1½–2 minutes or until tender. Turn back edge of plastic wrap; drain zucchini. Set aside.

3. Combine cottage cheese, mozzarella cheese, egg, and seasoning in small dish; mix well. Layer half of noodles in bottom of 6- by 6-inch microwave-safe baking dish. Top with half the tomato sauce, all the zucchini, and half the cheese mixture. Layer on remaining noodles, cheese mixture, and tomato sauce. Sprinkle with Parmesan cheese. Cover with waxed paper.

4. MICROWAVE (medium—50%) 6–8 minutes or until heated (150° F), rotating dish once. Let stand 5–10 minutes before cutting and serving.

TIPS

- If desired, double recipe and freeze one dish. Allow dish to thaw in refrigerator overnight, then heat as directed in step 4, increasing time to 7–8 minutes.

- To use full power instead of medium power in step 4, MICROWAVE 3 minutes and let stand 3 minutes. Then MICROWAVE 1–2 minutes or until hot.

QUICK CREAMY BEANS

**About 2 servings,
95 calories each**

A hint of dill adds flavor to this speedy sauce for favorite vegetables.

*1 10-ounce package frozen
   French-cut green beans*

2 tablespoons skim milk

1 tablespoon mayonnaise

¼ teaspoon dried dill weed

Dash salt and pepper

1. Place beans in 1-quart microwave-safe casserole. Cover with casserole lid.

2. MICROWAVE (high) 5–6 minutes or until just about tender. Drain.

3. Combine remaining ingredients; mix lightly with beans. Cover.

4. MICROWAVE (high) 1–2 minutes or until heated through.

This 435-calorie menu is perfect for a fall or winter evening. The meat loaf recipe makes 2 extra servings that you can refrigerate or freeze to enjoy for another quick meal. Cooking for one or two can be fun, especially when you can use new cooking dishes such as mugs and small casserole dishes.

MENU
INDIVIDUAL MEAT LOAVES
POTATOES AU GRATIN
SAVORY SQUASH

TIME GUIDE
About 30 minutes ahead:
Prepare Savory Squash, steps 1 and 2.
Prepare Potatoes au Gratin, steps 1 and 2.
Prepare Individual Meat Loaves, step 1.
Complete potatoes, step 3.
Complete meat loaves, step 2.
Complete squash, steps 3 and 4.

INDIVIDUAL MEAT LOAVES

About 4 servings, 175 calories each

A combination of ground turkey and beef is used in these flavorful individual loaves. Serve 2 now and freeze or refrigerate the other 2 for another meal.

¼ pound lean ground beef

½ pound ground turkey

3 tablespoons quick cooking rolled oats

3 tablespoons skim milk

2 tablespoons catsup

1 teaspoon Worcestershire sauce

¼ teaspoon onion powder

⅛ teaspoon pepper

4 teaspoons catsup

1. Combine all ingredients except 4 teaspoons catsup in mixing bowl; mix well. Divide into 4 equal portions. Wrap, label, and freeze 2 portions. Press other 2 portions into two 6- to 8-ounce microwave-safe mugs or custard cups. Spread each with 1 teaspoon catsup. Cover with waxed paper.

2. MICROWAVE (high) 2 loaves at a time 3–4 minutes or until no longer pink (150° F), rearranging mugs once. Let stand 5 minutes. Transfer to serving plate.

TIPS

- To microwave frozen meat loaves, allow mixture to stand in refrigerator overnight to thaw. Press into cups, top each with 1 teaspoon catsup, and MICROWAVE as directed.

- For one loaf, MICROWAVE 2½–3 minutes.

POTATOES AU GRATIN

**About 2 servings,
160 calories each**

Use a frozen hash brown patty to make this tasty potato dish. Convenience foods can help make small-quantity cooking quick yet very tasty.

1 frozen hash brown patty
   (about 6 ounces)

⅔ cup skim milk

1 teaspoon margarine

½ teaspoon instant minced
   onion

¼ teaspoon salt

Dash pepper

1 tablespoon grated Parmesan
   cheese

¼ teaspoon parsley flakes

Paprika

1. Combine hash brown patty, milk, margarine, onion, salt, and pepper in 1-quart microwave-safe casserole. Cover with casserole lid.

2. MICROWAVE (high) 4–5 minutes or until potatoes are partially thawed, stirring once. Stir in Parmesan cheese.

3. MICROWAVE (high) 4–5 minutes or until hot and bubbly, stirring once. Sprinkle with parsley and paprika.

TIP

● Other shallow microwave-safe casseroles or baking dishes that hold 3–4 cups can be used. If no casserole lid is available, cover dish with plastic wrap.

SAVORY SQUASH

**About 2 servings,
100 calories each**

Apple jelly adds sweetness, and marjoram adds a touch of interest to this autumn favorite.

1 small acorn squash

⅛ teaspoon salt

2 teaspoons margarine

2 teaspoons apple jelly

⅛ teaspoon dried marjoram
   leaves, crushed

1. Pierce squash with fork several times to allow steam to escape. Place stem side down on paper towel in microwave oven.

2. MICROWAVE (high) 5–7 minutes or until soft to the touch. Let stand 10 minutes.

3. Cut in half. Place cut side up on microwave-safe serving plate. Sprinkle with salt. Divide margarine, apple jelly, and marjoram between squash halves.

4. MICROWAVE (high), uncovered, 1½–2 minutes or until jelly is melted and squash is hot.

Cheeseburgers, oven fries, and green beans combine for a quick and easy meal with only 395 calories. It's perfect for those days when there is little time to prepare a meal, yet you want something warm and nutritious.

MENU
BACON CHEESEBURGERS
PARMESAN OVEN FRIES
LEMON-LITE GREEN BEANS

TIME GUIDE
About 20 minutes ahead:
Prepare Bacon Cheeseburgers, steps 1 and 2.
Prepare Lemon-Lite Green Beans.
Prepare Parmesan Oven Fries.
Complete burgers, steps 3 and 4.
Reheat beans if necessary.

BACON CHEESEBURGERS

**About 2 servings,
250 calories each**

It takes only a little bacon to add a delicious flavor to many foods. In the microwave oven, it is cooked between paper towels, which helps to eliminate much of the extra fat.

1 slice bacon

½ pound lean ground beef

Dash salt

Dash pepper

2 tablespoons shredded cheddar cheese

1. Layer bacon between paper towels on paper plate.

2. MICROWAVE (high) 45–90 seconds or until crisp. Cool and crumble bacon; set aside.

3. Season beef with salt and pepper. Form into 4 thin patties, about 3 inches in diameter. Sprinkle 2 patties with bacon. Top each with a plain patty, pressing edges together to seal. Place on microwave-safe meat rack. Cover with waxed paper.

4. MICROWAVE (high) 2–3 minutes or until no longer pink, rotating rack once. Sprinkle with cheese.

TIP

• Other favorite cheeses can be substituted for cheddar.

PARMESAN OVEN FRIES

About 2 servings, 110 calories each

Lightly seasoned potato wedges are sure to be a favorite to serve with many foods.

½ **tablespoon cooking oil**

1 **large baking potato (about 8 ounces)**

½ **tablespoon grated Parmesan cheese**

½ **teaspoon salad seasoning**

Dash salt

1. Place oil in 8-inch round microwave-safe baking dish. Scrub potato; cut in half lengthwise. Then cut each half into 6 wedges. Place wedges in dish, coating all sides of potato with oil. Combine Parmesan cheese, seasoning, and salt; sprinkle over potato wedges. Cover with paper towel.

2. MICROWAVE (high) 6–7 minutes or until potatoes are tender, rotating dish once.

LEMON-LITE GREEN BEANS

About 2 servings, 35 calories each

A touch of lemon adds zest to green beans.

1½ **cups frozen French-cut green beans**

1 **tablespoon water**

1 **teaspoon margarine**

¼ **teaspoon lemon juice**

Dash salt

Dash pepper

1. Combine beans and water in 20-ounce microwave-safe casserole. Cover with casserole lid.

2. MICROWAVE (high) 5–6 minutes or until tender. Drain. Stir in remaining ingredients.

It's possible to enjoy special dishes like beef stroganoff even when your family is small. This well-balanced meal adds up to only 445 calories. If you are cooking for only one person, spoon the other serving onto a microwave-safe plate and refrigerate to heat within a day or two.

MENU
STROGANOFF FOR TWO
POPPY SEED NOODLES
TARRAGON CARROTS AND ZUCCHINI

TIME GUIDE
About 30 minutes ahead:
Prepare Poppy Seed Noodles, steps 1 and 2.
Prepare Stroganoff for Two, steps 1-3.
Prepare Tarragon Carrots and Zucchini, steps 1 and 2.
Complete stroganoff, step 4.
Complete noodles, step 3.
Complete carrots, step 3.

STROGANOFF FOR TWO

**About 2 servings,
280 calories each**

Select a lean and tender cut of beef for this easy dish that makes a special dinner for two.

1 6-ounce boneless beef top sirloin steak, cut into ¼-inch strips

½ teaspoon natural meat browning and seasoning powder

1 cup (4 ounces) sliced fresh mushrooms

2 tablespoons chopped onion

1 tablespoon flour

1 teaspoon instant beef bouillon

2 tablespoons dry red wine (optional)

¼ cup water

¼ cup reduced-calorie sour cream

Snipped parsley

1. Place meat in 1½-quart microwave-safe casserole. Sprinkle with browning powder; toss to coat evenly. Add mushrooms and onion. Cover with casserole lid.

2. MICROWAVE (high) 3–3½ minutes or until meat is no longer pink, stirring once. Stir in flour, bouillon, wine, and water until blended.

3. MICROWAVE (high), uncovered, 2–3 minutes or until mixture boils and thickens, stirring once. Stir in sour cream. Cover.

4. MICROWAVE (high) 45–60 seconds or until heated through. Garnish with parsley.

TIPS

- If browning powder is not available, brown meat in a small amount of oil over medium heat. MICROWAVE as directed in steps 3 and 4.

- Plain yogurt can be substituted for reduced-calorie sour cream.

POPPY SEED NOODLES

**About 2 servings,
125 calories each**

Noodles make a nice accompaniment for Stroganoff as well as many other meat dishes. Since they reheat well, they can often be prepared toward the beginning of a meal and then reheated just before serving. Or, when time is especially short, cook the noodles conventionally while preparing the meat and vegetable in the microwave.

2 cups hot water

½ teaspoon salt

2 ounces uncooked medium egg noodles (about 1⅓ cups)

1 teaspoon margarine

¼ teaspoon poppy seed

1. MICROWAVE (high) water in uncovered 1-quart microwave-safe measure 4–5 minutes or until boiling. Stir in salt and noodles.

2. MICROWAVE (high), uncovered, 5–6 minutes or until noodles are just about tender. Let stand 5 minutes. Drain. Add margarine and poppy seed. Cover with plastic wrap.

3. MICROWAVE (high) 1–2 minutes or until heated through. Toss lightly to coat noodles.

TARRAGON CARROTS AND ZUCCHINI

**About 2 servings,
40 calories each**

Here is a colorful combination of vegetables with a tasty tarragon glaze.

½ cup sliced carrot

½ zucchini, cut into 1½- by ⅛- inch sticks

2 teaspoons water

1 teaspoon margarine

⅛ teaspoon dried tarragon leaves, crushed

1. Combine carrot, zucchini, and water in 20-ounce microwave-safe casserole. Cover with casserole lid or plastic wrap.

2. MICROWAVE (high) 1½–2 minutes or until just about tender. Let stand 5 minutes. Drain. Stir in margarine and tarragon.

3. MICROWAVE (high) 30–60 seconds or until heated.

This appealing menu includes a chicken-vegetable combination dish and rice for a total of 325 calories.

MENU
CHICKEN AND VEGGIE BUNDLES
RICE FOR TWO

TIME GUIDE
About 20 minutes ahead:
Prepare Chicken and Veggie Bundles, steps 1 and 2.
Prepare Rice for Two.
Complete chicken, steps 3–5.
Reheat rice if necessary.

CHICKEN AND VEGGIE BUNDLES

About 2 servings, 185 calories each

This colorful dish has a light sauce that goes nicely with rice or pasta.

4 ounces broccoli spears (about 3 inches long)

1 medium carrot, cut into sticks 2½ inches long

¼ cup water

1 teaspoon instant chicken bouillon

1 whole skinned and boned chicken breast (about 8 ounces), split

1 teaspoon natural chicken browning and seasoning powder

1 teaspoon Italian seasoning

1 teaspoon cornstarch

2 teaspoons water

1. Cut broccoli into even-sized spears. Arrange broccoli in 2 mounds in 10- by 6-inch microwave-safe baking dish, placing flower portion toward outside of dish. Top each with half the carrots. Add water and bouillon. Cover with plastic wrap, turning back a corner to allow excess steam to escape.

2. MICROWAVE (high) 1½–2 minutes or until bright-colored.

3. Place a chicken breast half on top of each vegetable mound, tucking ends under vegetables. Sprinkle with browning powder and Italian seasoning. Cover with plastic wrap.

4. MICROWAVE (high) 5–6 minutes or until chicken is done. Transfer chicken and vegetables to serving plate. Combine cornstarch and water; mix well. Blend into juices in baking dish.

5. MICROWAVE (high), uncovered, 1–2 minutes or until mixture boils and thickens, stirring once. Pour sauce over chicken.

TIPS

- If chicken breasts are not large enough to tuck under vegetables, flatten slightly by placing between sheets of plastic wrap and pounding with rolling pin.

- If browning powder is not available, sprinkle chicken with paprika.

RICE FOR TWO

**About 2 servings,
140 calories each**

This mildly seasoned rice is just the right accompaniment for many meals. These servings are about ³⁄₄-cup size; if you allow three ¹⁄₂-cup servings, calories will be only about 95 each.

¾ **cup water**

1 **teaspoon instant minced onion**

½ **teaspoon instant chicken bouillon**

¾ **cup quick-cooking white rice**

1. Combine water, onion, and bouillon in 1-quart microwave-safe casserole. Cover with casserole lid.

2. MICROWAVE (high) 2½–3 minutes or until mixture boils. Stir in rice. Cover and let stand 5 minutes. Fluff with fork.

The preparation time and cleanup are minimal in this tasty one-dish poultry dinner. Even with an extra vegetable, there are only 425 calories per serving.

MENU
PEASANT CHICKEN
ONION TOPPER TOMATOES

TIME GUIDE
About 25 minutes ahead:
Prepare Peasant Chicken.
Prepare Onion Topper Tomatoes.

PEASANT CHICKEN

**About 2 servings,
320 calories each**

You are sure to enjoy the flavors of this dish as well as the convenience of cooking the chicken, potato, and vegetable all in the same dish.

2 medium-size red potatoes, sliced thin

½ small onion, sliced thin

1 teaspoon instant chicken bouillon

2 tablespoons water

1 cup frozen French-cut green beans

1 teaspoon chopped pimiento

¼ teaspoon dried dill weed

1 whole skinned and boned chicken breast (about 12 ounces), halved

Natural chicken browning and seasoning powder

1. Combine potatoes, onion, bouillon, and water in 10- by 6-inch microwave-safe baking dish. Cover with plastic wrap.

2. MICROWAVE (high) 3–4 minutes or until potatoes are partially cooked. Stir. Top with green beans, pimiento, and dill weed. Arrange chicken on vegetables; sprinkle with browning powder. Cover with plastic wrap.

3. MICROWAVE (high) 8–10 minutes or until chicken and vegetables are done.

TIP

• If browning powder is not available, sprinkle chicken with paprika, salt, and pepper.

ONION TOPPER TOMATOES

**About 2 servings,
105 calories each**

Onion soup adds a savory accent to these fresh tomato halves.

2 medium tomatoes

*1 tablespoon dry onion soup
mix*

1 tablespoon margarine

1 tablespoon dry bread crumbs

1. Core tomatoes and cut each in half crosswise; arrange cut side up on microwave-safe serving plate. Sprinkle tomatoes with onion soup mix. Combine margarine and bread crumbs in small microwave-safe dish.

2. MICROWAVE (high) 30–40 seconds or until margarine is melted; mix lightly. Spoon onto tomatoes.

3. MICROWAVE (high), uncovered, 1½–2 minutes or until tomatoes are heated, rotating plate once.

This simple 400-calorie menu is ready to serve in about 20 minutes. Enjoy the soup while the chicken is in the final cooking step.

MENU
EGG DROP SOUP
CHICKEN STIR-FRY

TIME GUIDE
About 20 minutes ahead:
Prepare Chicken Stir-Fry, step 1.
Prepare Egg Drop Soup.
Complete chicken, steps 2 and 3.

EGG DROP SOUP

**About 2 servings,
70 calories each**

This delicious soup makes an easy accompaniment for Oriental or stir-fry dishes.

1 14½-ounce can chicken broth

Dash white pepper (optional)

1 medium green onion, sliced (including top)

1 egg, beaten

1. MICROWAVE (high) chicken broth and pepper in uncovered 4-cup microwave-safe measure 4–5 minutes or until boiling.

2. Stir green onion into egg; pour egg mixture slowly into broth, stirring constantly with fork until egg forms shreds.

TIP

- For a heartier soup, add 1 teaspoon finely chopped ham and a few chopped pea pods when heating broth.

CHICKEN STIR-FRY

**About 2 servings,
330 calories each**

Marinated chicken strips cook with frozen vegetables for a delicious entree.

1 **whole skinned and boned
chicken breast (about 12
ounces), split**

1 **tablespoon brown sugar**

3 **tablespoons soy sauce**

2 **tablespoons dry sherry**

1 **tablespoon cooking oil**

1 **clove garlic, minced**

Dash ground ginger

Dash pepper

½ **tablespoon cornstarch**

2 **cups frozen Japanese-style
vegetables**

1. Cut chicken into thin strips, about ½-inch thick and 2-inches long. Combine brown sugar, soy sauce, sherry, oil, garlic, ginger, and pepper in 1-quart microwave-safe mixing bowl. Add chicken; toss to coat. Let stand 10 minutes.

2. Stir in cornstarch; add vegetables. Cover with waxed paper.

3. MICROWAVE (high) 7–8 minutes or until chicken is done and sauce is thickened, stirring 2 or 3 times.

TIPS

- Sherry can be omitted; add ½ teaspoon lemon juice and 2 tablespoons water with brown sugar.

- If desired, serve with rice.

Here's a quick 25-minute dinner menu featuring fish. At 255 calories, you will want to repeat it often.

MENU
GOLDEN FISH NUGGETS
VEGETABLE MEDLEY

TIME GUIDE
About 25 minutes ahead:
Prepare Vegetable Medley.
Prepare Golden Fish Nuggets.

GOLDEN FISH NUGGETS

**About 2 servings,
120 calories each**

Turn ordinary fish into golden nuggets of goodness. It's an easy recipe that both children and adults will like.

1 tablespoon dry bread crumbs

1 tablespoon grated Parmesan cheese

1 teaspoon snipped chives

½ teaspoon paprika

Dash salt

8 ounces thick-cut cod fillets

1. Combine bread crumbs, Parmesan cheese, chives, paprika, and salt on waxed paper. Cut cod into nugget-size pieces; pat on paper towel to remove excess moisture. Roll in crumb mixture, coating all sides. Arrange in 8-inch round microwave-safe baking dish. Cover with paper towel.

2. MICROWAVE (high) 2½–3 minutes or until fish flakes apart easily.

TIPS

- Other firm-textured fish fillets can be substituted for cod.

- This crumb mixture also makes a good coating for chicken or turkey. Increase cooking time for chicken or turkey to 3½–4 minutes.

VEGETABLE MEDLEY

**About 2 servings,
135 calories each**

Potato, carrot, and celery team together in this flavorful vegetable dish.

*1 medium potato (about 6
ounces)*

1 small carrot, sliced thin

1 stalk celery, sliced thin

*3 green onions, sliced (including
tops)*

1 clove garlic, minced

1 tablespoon snipped parsley

2 tablespoons water

1 tablespoon margarine

⅛ teaspoon thyme leaves

Salt to taste (optional)

1. Scrub and slice potato into 1-quart microwave-safe casserole. Add remaining ingredients except margarine and thyme. Cover with casserole lid.

2. MICROWAVE (high) 6–7 minutes or until vegetables are tender-crisp, stirring once. Drain. Add margarine, thyme, and salt; cover.

3. MICROWAVE (high) 1–2 minutes or until vegetables are tender. Let stand about 5 minutes. Stir lightly to glaze vegetables. If desired, season with a little salt.

Enjoy this spicy fish dinner with only 425 calories. Fish cooks quickly in the microwave, but it seems even quicker when preparing small quantities. The meal is ready to eat in about 20 minutes.

MENU
FISH WITH CREOLE RICE
DILLED FRESH PEAS

TIME GUIDE
About 20 minutes ahead:
Prepare Fish with Creole Rice, steps 1-3.
Prepare Dilled Fresh Peas.
Complete fish, step 4.

FISH WITH CREOLE RICE

About 2 servings, 325 calories each

Fish combines with a spicy tomato and rice mixture for a colorful and flavorful dish.

¼ cup chopped green pepper

2 green onions, sliced (including tops)

1 tablespoon margarine

1 medium tomato, chopped

¼ teaspoon salt

¼ teaspoon chili powder

3 drops hot pepper sauce (optional)

¼ cup water

½ cup quick-cooking rice

8 ounces sole or other favorite fish fillets

1. Combine green pepper, onions, and margarine in 1-quart microwave-safe casserole.
2. MICROWAVE (high), uncovered, 1½–2 minutes or until tender. Add tomato, salt, chili powder, pepper sauce, and water. Cover with casserole lid.
3. MICROWAVE (high) 4–5 minutes or until boiling. Mix in rice. Lay fillets on rice. Cover.
4. MICROWAVE (high) 3–4 minutes or until fish flakes apart easily, rotating dish once. Let stand a few minutes before serving.

DILLED FRESH PEAS

**About 2 servings,
100 calories each**

Margarine and dill add a pleasant accent to fresh or frozen peas.

1 cup fresh shelled peas

2 tablespoons water

1 tablespoon margarine

⅛ teaspoon dried dill weed

1. Combine peas and water in 2-cup microwave-safe serving dish. Cover with plastic wrap or lid.

2. MICROWAVE (high) 3–3½ minutes or until tender. Drain. Add margarine and dill. Let stand a couple of minutes until margarine is melted; stir gently to coat.

TIPS

● Frozen peas can be substituted for fresh. Just measure 1 cup from a bag of "pourable" vegetables.

● Use the same seasonings with frozen peas and carrots.

Fish is a natural for lite dining and microwaves beautifully even in small quantities. Combined with spaghetti this menu adds up to only 340 calories. And it is all table-ready in about 20 minutes.

MENU
STUFFED DILLED SOLE
SPINACH SPAGHETTI

TIME GUIDE
About 20 minutes ahead:
Prepare Spinach Spaghetti, steps 1 and 2.
Prepare Stuffed Dilled Sole.
Complete spaghetti, step 3.

STUFFED DILLED SOLE

**About 2 servings,
170 calories each**

Julienne strips of carrot and zucchini are rolled inside sole fillets.

8 ounces sole or other favorite fish fillets

Salt

1 small carrot, cut into 1½- by ⅛-inch sticks

1 small zucchini, cut into 1½- by ¼-inch sticks

2 tablespoons plain yogurt

1 tablespoon mayonnaise

⅛ teaspoon dill weed

1. Cut fillets, if necessary, into 2 serving-size pieces. Sprinkle with salt. Divide vegetables between fillets. Roll up fillets with vegetables inside, starting at narrow end. Secure with toothpick if necessary. Place seam side down in shallow microwave-safe baking dish. Cover with plastic wrap.

2. MICROWAVE (high) 3–4 minutes or until fish flakes apart easily, rotating dish once. Set aside. Combine yogurt, mayonnaise, and dill weed until blended. Spoon onto fish.

3. MICROWAVE (high), uncovered, 30–60 seconds or until sauce is heated.

SPINACH SPAGHETTI

About 2 servings,
170 calories each

Colorful spaghetti adds interest to less colorful entrees. Be sure not to overcook this type of pasta, or it can become very pasty.

4 cups hot water

½ teaspoon salt

3 ounces spinach spaghetti

1 tablespoon margarine

1 tablespoon Parmesan cheese

1. MICROWAVE (high) water and salt in uncovered 2-quart microwave-safe mixing bowl 5–6 minutes or until steaming hot. Add spaghetti.

2. MICROWAVE (high), uncovered, 3–4 minutes or until just about tender, stirring once. Let stand 5 minutes. Drain. Add margarine and Parmesan cheese.

3. MICROWAVE (high), uncovered, 1–2 minutes or until heated through.

Serve this 300-calorie menu for a special occasion to be shared or celebrated by two. Not only is it easy to prepare, but it also will be sure to add to the occasion at hand. The preparation takes less than 25 minutes! To make it even quicker, have the rice cooked ahead and just reheat it for serving.

MENU
SHRIMP SCAMPI
QUICK RICE PILAF

TIME GUIDE
About 25 minutes ahead:
Prepare Quick Rice Pilaf
Prepare Shrimp Scampi.

SHRIMP SCAMPI

**About 2 servings,
135 calories each**

A lite garlic sauce glazes this shrimp and vegetable dish. It is as tasty as it is pretty.

1 clove garlic, minced

1 tablespoon margarine

*8 ounces frozen uncooked large
shrimp, rinsed and drained*

½ cup fresh pea pods

2 tablespoons snipped parsley

½ teaspoon cornstarch

½ teaspoon lemon juice

Dash salt

6 cherry tomatoes, halved

1. MICROWAVE (high) garlic and margarine in uncovered 8-inch round microwave-safe baking dish 1½–2 minutes or until tender. Mix in shrimp, pea pods, and parsley. Cover with waxed paper.

2. MICROWAVE (high) 4–4½ minutes or until shrimp are firm and opaque, stirring once or twice. Drain juice from shrimp into 1-cup microwave-safe measure. Stir in cornstarch, lemon juice, and salt, blending well.

3. MICROWAVE (high), uncovered, 45–60 seconds or until mixture boils and thickens, stirring once. Pour mixture over shrimp; add tomatoes.

4. MICROWAVE (high), uncovered, 1–1½ minutes or until heated through.

TIP

- Half a package of frozen pea pods can be substituted for fresh. Rinse under water to thaw partially before adding in step 1.

QUICK RICE PILAF

**About 2 servings,
165 calories each**

This is so easy to prepare that you'll want to serve it often. Cook it right in the same dish you will use for serving and save on cleanup, too.

1 *teaspoon margarine*

1 *green onion, sliced (including top)*

¾ *cup water*

1 *teaspoon instant chicken bouillon*

¾ *cup quick-cooking rice*

½ *teaspoon parsley flakes*

1 *tablespoon slivered almonds*

1. MICROWAVE (high) margarine and green onion in uncovered 1-quart microwave-safe casserole 45–60 seconds or until tender. Add water and bouillon. Cover with casserole lid.

2. MICROWAVE (high) 2½–3 minutes or until mixture boils. Add rice and parsley. Cover and let stand 5 minutes. Fluff with fork. Sprinkle with almonds.

Dinner for two can be elegant, and this 395-calorie menu proves it. Serve it for any special occasion. With calories this low, you can even include a favorite dessert! With recipes such as these, where all foods cook in about the same time, it is easiest to cook each partially and then complete the cooking. This way, all foods are still hot when ready to serve.

MENU
STEAK DIANE
LO-CAL BAKED POTATOES
GREEN BEAN-FILLED TOMATOES

TIME GUIDE
About 30 minutes ahead:
Prepare Steak Diane, steps 1 and 2.
Prepare Lo-Cal Baked Potatoes, steps 1 and 2.
Prepare Green Bean-Filled Tomatoes, steps 1-3.
Complete meat, steps 3 and 4.
Complete tomatoes, step 4.
Complete potatoes, steps 3 and 4.

STEAK DIANE

**About 2 servings,
265 calories each**

In this recipe, a special microwave browning dish is used to brown the meat while the microwaves cook it quickly without drying.

1 8-ounce boneless top sirloin or round tip steak, cut ½-inch thick

½ cup sliced fresh mushrooms

2 teaspoons Worcestershire sauce

1 tablespoon margarine

2 green onions, chopped (including tops)

1 teaspoon snipped parsley

1 teaspoon lemon juice

⅛ teaspoon dry mustard

⅛ teaspoon garlic powder

1 teaspoon cooking oil

1. Trim fat from steak. Cut into 2 pieces. Pound each between sheets of plastic wrap with meat mallet or rolling pin until ¼-inch thick. Combine mushrooms, Worcestershire sauce, margarine, onions, parsley, lemon juice, mustard, and garlic powder in 1-cup microwave-safe measure.

2. MICROWAVE (high), uncovered, 1½-2 minutes or until vegetables are tender. Set aside.

3. Preheat browning dish 5-8 minutes or as directed by manufacturer for cooking meat. Coat dish lightly with oil. Place steaks on hot dish.

4. MICROWAVE (high), uncovered, 1 minute. Turn meat over. Then MICROWAVE (high) 30-60 seconds or until desired doneness. Drain juices into vegetable mixture; mix well. Serve sauce over steaks.

TIP

• If browning dish is not available, cook steaks under broiler or on barbecue grill.

LO-CAL BAKED POTATOES

**About 2 servings,
55 calories each**

Reduced-calorie sour cream and a touch of Italian seasoning are the secret ingredients in these potatoes that taste almost like the higher-calorie version.

1 **large baking potato (about 8 ounces)**

2 **tablespoons reduced-calorie sour cream**

¼ **teaspoon Italian salad seasoning**

Dash salt

Dash pepper

1. Scrub potato; pierce several times with fork.
2. MICROWAVE (high) 3½–4½ minutes or until just about tender, turning potato over once. Let stand about 5 minutes.
3. Combine sour cream and salad seasoning in small bowl. Cut potato in half lengthwise. Press sides lightly to loosen potato. Place on microwave-safe serving plate. Sprinkle with salt and pepper. Spoon sour cream mixture onto each potato half.
4. MICROWAVE (high), uncovered, 45–60 seconds or until hot.

TIP

● Snipped chives and a little garlic salt can be substituted for salad seasoning.

GREEN BEAN–FILLED TOMATOES

**About 2 servings,
75 calories each**

Combining vegetables results in interesting flavors and adds delightful color to brighten any meal. Tomatoes, either whole or halves, make such nice holders for other vegetables that you will want to try this idea with other favorites, too.

**2 medium-size firm ripe
   tomatoes**

Salt

**1 cup frozen French-cut green
   beans**

1 teaspoon margarine

1 teaspoon dry bread crumbs

**1 teaspoon grated Parmesan
   cheese**

⅛ teaspoon dried basil leaves

Dash pepper

1. Cut top off each tomato. Carefully scoop out pulp, leaving about ¼-inch of tomato. Sprinkle insides lightly with salt. Place upside down on paper toweling to drain.

2. MICROWAVE (high) green beans in covered 1-cup microwave-safe measure 1–1½ minutes or until hot. Place tomatoes cut side up on microwave-safe serving plate. Spoon beans into tomatoes.

3. MICROWAVE (high) margarine in uncovered 1-cup microwave-safe measure 30–45 seconds or until melted. Stir in remaining ingredients. Sprinkle over beans. Cover with waxed paper.

4. MICROWAVE (high) 2½–3 minutes or until tomatoes are hot, rotating plate once.

TIP

- If you have large tomatoes on hand, use 1 instead of 2 and halve crosswise instead of cutting off top, then scoop out pulp. Fill and heat as directed.

CHAPTER
6
QUICK AND EASY MEALS

Only a few minutes to spare at mealtime? Browse through the following pages for table-ready meal ideas to be made in 30 minutes or less. You'll find a variety of menus, perfect for dinner, supper, or lunch.

For some quick and easy meal preparation, we have teamed the conventional range with the microwave. Cooking pasta on a surface unit while the microwave is used for a sauce and accompaniments is one example.

The following menus range from 190 to 440 calories. Some fairly basic convenience foods have been used to speed the preparation. Most recipes, though, use ingredients that would commonly be found on your cupboard shelves.

To help make these recipes quick, we use tender, quick-cooking cuts of meat, frozen precut vegetables, quick-cooking rice, and canned and frozen fruits. Many of the dishes are stirred since this helps them to heat more quickly. Individual servings cook faster than a larger container, and you will find some of these types of recipes, too. Also, many of the entrees incorporate meat, vegetable, and pasta in one dish to save you valuable time and make cleanup easy.

Microwave ovens are often purchased for the speed and convenience they offer. These meals and recipes will help you maximize your microwave's usefulness and discover the quick and easy cooking that is possible when minutes count.

This menu features an interesting combination of vegetables, pasta, and turkey served with a refreshing fruit salad. With one-dish dinners like this, you need only a salad or relishes. One of the best features of this meal is that it adds up to only 415 calories!

MENU
TURKEY-PASTA TOSS
LITE YOGURT SALAD

TIME GUIDE
About 30 minutes ahead:
Prepare Lite Yogurt Salad, steps 1 and 2.
Prepare Turkey-Pasta Toss.
Complete salad, step 3.

TURKEY-PASTA TOSS

**About 5 servings,
305 calories each**

For this easy one-dish meal, meat, vegetable, and pasta are all served in one colorful combination. To speed the preparation, the pasta is cooked conventionally while the turkey and vegetables are prepared in the microwave.

6 ounces linguine noodles

12 ounces boneless turkey

1 clove garlic, minced

2 green onions, sliced

1 tablespoon margarine

2 cups sliced zucchini

2 cups sliced yellow summer squash

1 cup (4 ounces) sliced fresh mushrooms

¼ cup skim milk

1 teaspoon cornstarch

¼ cup grated Parmesan cheese

¼ teaspoon salt

1. Cook linguine as directed on package. Drain and rinse in cold water. Set aside.

2. Cut turkey into thin strips, about ¼-inch thick. Combine turkey, garlic, onions, and margarine in 2-quart microwave-safe casserole. Cover with casserole lid.

3. MICROWAVE (high) 4–4½ minutes or until no longer pink, stirring once.

4. Add zucchini, squash, and mushrooms to turkey. Cover.

5. MICROWAVE (high) 6–7 minutes or until tender-crisp. Combine milk, cornstarch, Parmesan cheese, and salt; mix well. Stir into vegetables. Add linguine. Cover.

6. MICROWAVE (high) 3–3½ minutes or until sauce boils and thickens slightly, stirring once.

TIPS

• Chicken can be substituted for turkey.

• Other favorite fresh vegetables can be substituted for zucchini. Just be sure they are all fairly quick-cooking.

LITE YOGURT SALAD

**About 5 servings,
110 calories each**

This dressing contains no added sugar or honey.

- **1 (8-ounce) can pineapple chunks in fruit juice**
- **1 tablespoon lemon juice**
- **1 egg, beaten**
- **1½ teaspoons cornstarch**
- **⅓ cup vanilla yogurt**
- **1 apple, sliced**
- **1 banana, sliced**
- **1 orange, peeled, sectioned and cut into pieces**

1. Drain pineapple juice into 2-cup microwave-safe measure. Add lemon juice, egg, and cornstarch; mix until smooth.

2. MICROWAVE (high), uncovered, 2½–3 minutes or until mixture boils and thickens, stirring twice. Refrigerate about 15 minutes to chill.

3. Mix in yogurt. Combine pineapple, apple, banana, orange, and dressing in serving bowl. Toss lightly to coat. Refrigerate until served.

There are 325 calories in this easy meal featuring an all-in-one turkey entree. Add a salad like this easy coleslaw, for color and texture. When time is short, prepare the slaw the night before.

MENU
TURKEY CLUB CASSEROLE
HOT SLAW

TIME GUIDE
About 30 minutes ahead:
Prepare Hot Slaw, steps 1 and 2.
Prepare Turkey Club Casserole.
Complete slaw, step 3.

TURKEY CLUB CASSEROLE

**About 6 servings,
190 calories each**

Bits of bacon, sliced tomato, and a lite cheese sauce transform turkey "planned overs" into a satisfying dish that you can serve for brunch, lunch, or supper.

2 slices bacon

2 tablespoons margarine

2 tablespoons flour

½ teaspoon instant chicken bouillon

1 cup skim milk

¼ cup shredded cheddar cheese

1½ cups cubed toasted wheat bread (about 3 slices)

1½ cups cubed cooked turkey or chicken

1 medium tomato, sliced thin

1 tablespoon snipped chives

1. Layer bacon between paper towels on paper plate.
2. MICROWAVE (high) 1½–2 minutes or until crisp; set aside.
3. MICROWAVE (high) margarine in uncovered 2-cup microwave-safe measure 30–45 seconds or until melted. Blend in flour and bouillon; stir in milk.
4. MICROWAVE (high), uncovered, 2½–3½ minutes or until mixture boils and thickens, stirring twice. Stir in cheese; set aside.
5. Layer toast cubes in bottom of 10- by 6-inch microwave-safe baking dish. Top with turkey and tomato. Pour cheese sauce evenly over all. Crumble bacon and sprinkle evenly over sauce.
6. MICROWAVE (high), uncovered, 3–4 minutes or until bubbly and heated through (150° F), rotating dish once. Sprinkle with chives.

TIPS

• About 2 tablespoons bacon-flavored bits can be substituted for cooked bacon.

• Other varieties of cheese can be substituted for cheddar.

HOT SLAW

**About 6 servings,
135 calories each**

A cabbage salad with an old-fashioned vinaigrette dressing. Refrigerate any leftovers and enjoy for several weeks.

4 cups shredded cabbage

1–2 tablespoons chopped onion

⅓ cup sugar

⅓ cup white vinegar

¼ cup cooking oil

1 teaspoon celery seed

½ teaspoon salt

¼ teaspoon dry mustard

1. Combine cabbage and onion in bowl or casserole; set aside.

2. Combine sugar, vinegar, oil, celery seed, salt, and dry mustard in 2-cup microwave-safe measure.

3. MICROWAVE (high), uncovered, 1½–2 minutes or until mixture boils and sugar is dissolved, stirring once. Pour over cabbage; mix lightly. If desired, cover tightly and refrigerate overnight. Salad can be stored in refrigerator for up to 2 weeks.

TIP

• Chopped green pepper can be added to onion.

Children are sure to enjoy this easy 370-calorie meal. The preparation is so easy that they can even help with much of it.

MENU
CHICKEN NUGGETS
TACO POTATO WEDGES

TIME GUIDE
About 30 minutes ahead:
Prepare Taco Potato Wedges.
Prepare Chicken Nuggets.
Reheat potatoes if necessary.

CHICKEN NUGGETS

**About 4 servings,
250 calories each**

Make homemade chicken nuggets quickly and easily in your microwave. Dip in honey, barbecue sauce, or applesauce for extra flavor. Cut the pieces as uniform as possible to aid even cooking. If some pieces are smaller, place them in the center of the baking dish.

1 pound skinned and boned chicken breast

3 tablespoons skim milk

3 tablespoons grated Parmesan cheese

3 tablespoons dry bread crumbs

½ teaspoon seasoned salt

¼ teaspoon paprika

⅛ teaspoon pepper

1. Cut chicken into 1-inch cubes. Place pieces in small bowl. Pour milk over chicken; mix lightly to coat evenly.

2. Combine remaining ingredients in plastic bag; mix lightly. Add half the chicken pieces to bag; shake to coat evenly. Transfer pieces to 9-inch microwave-safe pie plate. Coat remaining pieces and place in pie plate. Cover with paper towel.

3. MICROWAVE (high) 7–8 minutes or until chicken is done, rotating plate once. If desired, serve with favorite dipping sauce.

TIPS

● Seasoned bread crumbs can be substituted for regular crumbs. Reduce salt to ¼ teaspoon.

● Boneless turkey can be substituted for chicken.

TACO POTATO WEDGES

**About 4 servings,
120 calories each**

These taco-flavored potato wedges are ready in a jiffy. They also make great snacks.

2 tablespoons margarine

**1–2 teaspoons taco seasoning
mix**

**2 large potatoes (about 16
ounces)**

1. MICROWAVE (high) margarine in uncovered 8-inch round microwave-safe baking dish 30–60 seconds or until melted. Stir in seasoning.

2. Scrub potatoes. Cut each in half lengthwise; then cut each half into 4 wedges. Coat wedges in margarine mixture as they are arranged in dish skin side down. Cover with plastic wrap.

3. MICROWAVE (high) 8–10 minutes or until potatoes are tender, rotating dish once.

TIP

● For other flavor variations, substitute dry salad dressing mixes for taco seasoning.

Filled baked potatoes can be the center of many quick meals. Just change the filling mixture and you have a new meal. Combined with an easy vegetable, these add up to just 330 calories. Add a tossed salad and/or bagel to complete the meal.

MENU
CHICKEN-STUFFED POTATOES
CHEESY VEGETABLES

TIME GUIDE
About 25 minutes ahead:
Prepare Chicken-Stuffed Potatoes, steps 1-4.
Prepare Cheesy Vegetables, steps 1 and 2.
Complete potatoes, step 5.
Complete vegetables, steps 3-5.

CHICKEN-STUFFED POTATOES

About 4 servings, 280 calories each

Don't let the number of steps in this recipe fool you; these potatoes are easy and delicious.

4 medium baking potatoes (about 2 pounds)

¾ cup sliced fresh mushrooms

1 tablespoon margarine

¾ cup water

1 green onion, sliced

1 tablespoon dry sherry

1 tablespoon cornstarch

1 tablespoon chopped pimiento

1 teaspoon instant chicken bouillon

⅛ teaspoon salt

1½ cups cubed cooked chicken

Salt to taste (optional)

1. Scrub potatoes; pierce each several times with fork. Arrange spoke-fashion in oven.

2. MICROWAVE (high) 14–16 minutes or until just about tender, turning potatoes over once. Let stand about 10 minutes. Combine mushrooms and margarine in 4-cup microwave-safe measure.

3. MICROWAVE (high), uncovered, 2–3 minutes or until tender. Stir in remaining ingredients, mixing until smooth.

4. MICROWAVE (high), uncovered, 5½–6½ minutes or until mixture boils and thickens, stirring once. Make a lengthwise cut down center of each potato, cutting almost through; press sides to open potatoes. Sprinkle with salt, if desired. Place potatoes on microwave-safe serving plate. Spoon chicken mixture into each potato.

5. MICROWAVE (high), uncovered, 3–4 minutes or until heated.

CHEESY VEGETABLES

**About 4 servings,
50 calories each**

We often throw away the thick broccoli stalks, forgetting they can be chopped and used to extend frozen vegetables with sauce.

1½ **cups peeled and chopped broccoli stalks (¼-inch pieces)**

2 **tablespoons water**

1 **10-ounce package frozen cauliflower in cheese sauce**

1. Combine broccoli and water in 1-quart microwave-safe casserole. Cover with casserole lid.

2. MICROWAVE (high) 5–6 minutes or until just about tender. Drain and set aside.

3. Make a slit in frozen vegetable pouch.

4. MICROWAVE (high) 4–4½ minutes or until thawed. Add to broccoli pieces; mix lightly. Cover.

5. MICROWAVE (high) 2–2½ minutes or until heated through and desired doneness.

TIPS

● For special occasions, top with buttered bread crumbs, adding a sprinkle of paprika to enhance the color.

● Other favorite vegetables in cheese sauce can be used.

Vegetable-topped fish, cooked cabbage, and cheesy apples make up this menu of only 265 calories. Fish is usually one of the last items cooked for a meal since it cooks so quickly.

MENU
COD BELLA VISTA
CABBAGE MEDLEY
APPLES AND CHEESE

TIME GUIDE
About 30 minutes ahead:
Prepare Apples and Cheese.
Prepare Cod Bella Vista, steps 1 and 2.
Prepare Cabbage Medley.
Complete cod, steps 3 and 4.

COD BELLA VISTA

**About 4 servings,
150 calories each**

Green pepper, onion, and tomato slices top cod or torsk for a lite and colorful entree.

1 pound cod or torsk fillets

2 tablespoons margarine

1 small onion, chopped

2 tablespoons dry white wine

¼ teaspoon salt

Dash pepper

1 small green pepper, chopped

1 medium tomato

1 tablespoon grated Parmesan cheese

1. Cut fish into 4 serving pieces; place in 10- by 6-inch microwave-safe baking dish. Place margarine and onion in 2-cup microwave-safe measure.

2. MICROWAVE (high), uncovered, 1–1½ minutes or until onion is just about tender. Stir in wine, salt, and pepper. Sprinkle green pepper over fish. Top with onion mixture. Cover with plastic wrap.

3. MICROWAVE (high) 3 minutes. Cut tomato into 4 slices; top each piece fish with a slice. Sprinkle with Parmesan cheese. Cover.

4. MICROWAVE (high) 2–3 minutes or until fish flakes apart easily with fork.

CABBAGE MEDLEY

**About 4 servings,
60 calories each**

Cabbage is low in calories and high in nutrients. It cooks beautifully in the microwave as you will see in this flavorful combination.

½ **medium head cabbage,
shredded (about 3 cups)**

1 **small onion, sliced**

½ **green pepper, chopped**

1 **tablespoon chopped pimiento**

1 **tablespoon margarine**

½ **teaspoon salt**

½ **teaspoon dill weed**

Dash pepper

1. Combine all ingredients in 1-quart microwave-safe casserole. Cover with casserole lid.

2. MICROWAVE (high) 5–6 minutes or until cabbage is tender-crisp, stirring once.

APPLES AND CHEESE

**About 4 servings,
55 calories each**

This simple but tasty way to serve apples is sure to be a favorite any time of the day.

1 **ounce Neufchâtel cheese**

1 **tablespoon shredded cheddar
cheese**

⅛ **teaspoon lemon juice**

2 **apples, cored and cut into
wedges**

Ground cinnamon

1. MICROWAVE (high) Neufchâtel cheese in uncovered microwave-safe custard cup 20–30 seconds or until softened. Stir in cheddar cheese and lemon juice.

2. Spread cheese mixture on one side of apple wedges. Sprinkle with cinnamon.

TIP

- If apples are prepared ahead, dip slices into lemon juice to prevent browning, then spread with cheese mixture.

This quick meal is special enough for company, too. Scallops cook quickly and go well with many different accompaniments. The scallops and beans add up to 220 calories. For heartier appetites, serve with rice.

MENU
SCALLOPS SUPREME
SAVORY ITALIAN GREEN BEANS

TIME GUIDE
About 20 minutes ahead:
Prepare Scallops Supreme, step 1.
Prepare Savory Italian Green Beans.
Complete scallops, steps 2–4.
Reheat beans if necessary.

SCALLOPS SUPREME

**About 4 servings,
170 calories each**

Scallops are ideal for quick meals as well as lite dining. This sauce, with a hint of wine, finishes them to perfection.

1 tablespoon lemon juice

2 tablespoons dry white wine

¼ teaspoon salt

⅛ teaspoon white pepper

1 pound fresh or thawed frozen scallops

2 teaspooons cornstarch

1 tablespoon margarine

2 tablespoons dry bread crumbs

⅛ teaspoon paprika

2 tablespoons snipped parsley

1. Combine lemon juice, wine, salt, and pepper in 8-inch round microwave-safe baking dish; blend well. Add scallops in single layer. Cover with waxed paper.

2. MICROWAVE (high) 4–5 minutes or until scallops are set, stirring once. Drain juices into 1-cup microwave-safe measure. Blend in cornstarch.

3. MICROWAVE (high), uncovered, 45–60 seconds or until mixture boils and thickens, stirring once. Pour over scallops. Set aside.

4. MICROWAVE (high) margarine in uncovered 1-cup microwave-safe measure 30–45 seconds or until melted. Stir in bread crumbs and paprika. Sprinkle on scallops; top with parsley.

TIP

• Water can be substituted for wine.

SAVORY ITALIAN GREEN BEANS

**About 4 servings,
50 calories each**

Savory adds a pleasant seasoning to Italian-cut beans.

1 **10-ounce package frozen
   Italian-cut green beans**

1 **teaspoon instant minced
   onion**

1 **tablespoon margarine**

1 **teaspoon chopped pimiento**

1 **teaspoon dried summer
   savory**

½ **teaspoon seasoned salt**

1. Combine beans, onion, margarine, and pimiento in 1-quart microwave-safe casserole. Cover with casserole lid.

2. MICROWAVE (high) 7–8 minutes or until beans are tender, stirring once. Stir in savory and salt.

Frozen vegetables help to make this meal quick and easy at only 190 calories.

MENU
TUNA-VEGETABLE CASSEROLE
BACON-TOPPED TOMATO SLICES

TIME GUIDE
About 30 minutes ahead:
Prepare Bacon-Topped Tomato Slices.
Prepare Tuna-Vegetable Casserole.

TUNA-VEGETABLE CASSEROLE

**About 6 servings,
160 calories each**

Tuna is combined with vegetables instead of pasta for a leaner version of a traditional favorite.

1 16-ounce package frozen vegetable combination (peas, cauliflower, and carrots)

1 6½-ounce can water-packed tuna, drained

1 4-ounce can sliced mushrooms, undrained

1 10¾-ounce can condensed mushroom soup

1 tablespoon instant minced onion

½ cup chow mein noodles

1. Combine all ingredients except noodles in 2-quart microwave-safe casserole. Cover with casserole lid.

2. MICROWAVE (high) 14–16 minutes or until mixture is hot and vegetables are tender, stirring once or twice. Top with noodles.

TIPS

- Other frozen vegetable combinations can be used. Or make your own combination with fresh vegetables that cook in about the same time.

- Cheddar cheese soup can be substituted for mushroom soup.

BACON-TOPPED TOMATO SLICES

**About 6 servings,
30 calories each**

You'll want to serve this recipe often when fresh tomatoes are plentiful.

2 slices bacon

2 medium tomatoes, sliced

1½ tablespoons lite Italian
dressing

⅛ teaspoon dried basil leaves

1. Layer bacon between paper towels on paper plate.

2. MICROWAVE (high) 1½–2½ minutes or until bacon is crisp, rotating plate once. Cool and crumble bacon.

3. Arrange tomato slices on serving plate. Drizzle dressing over tomatoes; sprinkle with basil and crumbled bacon. Refrigerate until served.

TIPS

- Bacon-flavored bits can be substituted for bacon; use about 1 tablespoon.

- If desired, tomatoes can be warmed by microwaving 45–60 seconds after topping with the bacon.

This quick menu features individual salmon loaves and broccoli. At only 280 total calories, it is sure to be an often-requested dinner.

MENU
SALMON TIMBALES WITH CUCUMBER SAUCE
BROCCOLI AMANDINE

TIME GUIDE
About 30 minutes ahead:
Prepare Broccoli Amandine, steps 1-3.
Prepare Salmon Timbales with Cucumber Sauce.
Complete broccoli, step 4.

SALMON TIMBALES WITH CUCUMBER SAUCE

About 4 servings, 235 calories each

These individual salmon loaves are flavored with lemon and dill and topped with a tasty cucumber sauce.

1 15-ounce can pink salmon, drained

2 slices bread, cubed

1 egg, beaten

½ cup shredded carrot

⅓ cup skim milk

1 tablespoon lemon juice

1 teaspoon parsley flakes

¼ teaspoon salt

Dash pepper

Sauce

¼ cup plain yogurt

⅓ cup chopped cucumber

½ teaspoon sugar

⅛ teaspoon dill weed

2 tablespoons chopped ripe olives (optional)

1. Remove skin and larger bones from salmon. Add bread, egg, carrot, milk, lemon juice, parsley, salt, and pepper; mix well. Spoon into four 6-ounce microwave-safe custard cups, packing evenly. Cover with waxed paper.

2. MICROWAVE (high) 6½–7½ minutes or until set, rearranging once. Combine sauce ingredients in small bowl. Invert salmon timbales onto serving plate. Top with sauce.

BROCCOLI AMANDINE

**About 4 servings,
45 calories each**

Microwaved vegetables taste so good that you can serve them with the simplest of toppings. Here we use toasted almonds with a touch of lemon . . . delicious!

1 tablespoon sliced almonds

1 tablespoon margarine

½ teaspoon lemon juice

8 ounces broccoli

2 tablespoons water

1. Combine almonds and margarine in 1-cup microwave-safe measure.

2. MICROWAVE (high), uncovered, 2½–3½ minutes or until lightly browned, stirring 2 or 3 times. Stir in lemon juice; set aside.

3. Cut broccoli into spears about 3 inches long and ½ inch thick. Arrange in shallow 1-quart microwave-safe casserole. Add water. Cover with casserole lid.

4. MICROWAVE (high) 4–5 minutes or until tender-crisp. Let stand about 3 minutes; drain. Top with almond mixture.

TIPS

- Serve this almond mixture on other favorite vegetables such as asparagus, green beans, or pea pods.

- A 10-ounce package of frozen broccoli spears can be substituted for fresh. Increase time in step 4 to 5–6 minutes.

Pizza-flavored pork patties combine with a delicious spinach salad for just 230 calories. While the patties are cooking, you can fix the salad and set the table. It's a delicious family or company dinner that you are sure to enjoy preparing, too.

MENU
PORK TENDERLOIN PATTIES
QUICK SPINACH SALAD

TIME GUIDE
About 30 minutes ahead:
Prepare Pork Tenderloin Patties, steps 1 and 2.
Prepare Quick Spinach Salad, steps 1 and 2.
Complete pork, steps 3 and 4.
Complete salad, step 3.

PORK TENDERLOIN PATTIES

**About 5 servings,
185 calories each**

The natural tenderness of pork makes it ideal for microwave cooking. These quick-cooking patties are finished with a pizza-like topping.

5 pork tenderloin patties (about 1 pound)

Water

Natural meat browning and seasoning powder

5 thin slices onion

1 cup pizza sauce (about 8 ounces)

½ cup (2 ounces) shredded mozzarella cheese

1. Arrange unrolled patties in single layer in 8- by 8-inch microwave-safe baking dish. Moisten with water; sprinkle with browning powder. Cover with waxed paper.

2. MICROWAVE (high) 5–6 minutes or until meat is no longer pink, rotating dish once. Drain.

3. Top each patty with onion slice and about 3 tablespoons sauce. Cover.

4. MICROWAVE (high) 8–10 minutes or until meat is tender, rotating dish once. Sprinkle with cheese; let stand, covered, 5 minutes.

TIP

● If tenderloin patties are not available, slice 1 pound pork tenderloin into 5 slices.

QUICK SPINACH SALAD

**About 5 servings,
45 calories each**

A warm dressing with sweet-sour flavors lightly coats fresh spinach in this salad.

*4 cups torn spinach leaves
(about 4 ounces)*

½ cup chopped cucumber

5 cherry tomatoes, halved

2 tablespoons sugar

2 tablespoons plain yogurt

*2 tablespoons mayonnaise or
salad dressing*

1 tablespoon white vinegar

1. Combine spinach, cucumber, and tomatoes in salad bowl; cover and refrigerate.

2. Mix together sugar, yogurt, mayonnaise, and vinegar in 1-cup microwave-safe measure.

3. MICROWAVE (high), uncovered, 1–1½ minutes or until mixture is boiling hot. Stir and immediately pour over spinach; toss to coat.

TIPS

- Crumbled cooked bacon can be added. Or use about 1 tablespoon bacon-flavored bits.

- Dressing is good on other types of tossed salads or vegetable combinations.

A fresh fruit combination is all that is needed to make a complete meal with this quick entree. This menu is colorful, simple, and very good for only 310 calories.

MENU
PORK LO MEIN
ORIENTAL FRUIT COMPOTE

TIME GUIDE
About 30 minutes ahead:
Prepare Pork Lo Mein, steps 1 and 2.
Prepare Oriental Fruit Compote.
Complete pork, steps 3 and 4.

PORK LO MEIN

**About 6 servings,
255 calories each**

This quick and easy version of a one-dish Chinese favorite includes meat, vegetables, and pasta. To save time, the spaghetti is cooked conventionally while the remainder is cooking in the microwave.

4 ounces thin spaghetti, broken into 3-inch lengths

1 pound boneless pork loin, cut into thin strips

¼ cup soy sauce

3 tablespoons cornstarch

2 tablespoons dry sherry or white wine

1 teaspoon sugar

1 16-ounce package frozen vegetable combination (broccoli, carrots, water chestnuts, and peppers)

¾ cup water

½ teaspoon instant chicken bouillon

1. Cook spaghetti as directed on package. Drain and rinse in cold water.

2. Combine pork, soy sauce, cornstarch, sherry, and sugar in 2-quart microwave-safe casserole; mix well. Cover with casserole lid. Let stand 5 minutes to marinate. Stir in vegetables, water, and bouillon. Cover.

3. MICROWAVE (high) 9–13 minutes or until vegetables are cooked and mixture is slightly thickened, stirring once. Add spaghetti; mix lightly. Cover.

4. MICROWAVE (high) 2–3 minutes or until heated through.

TIPS

- Lite pasta or rice noodles can be substituted for spaghetti.

- Other vegetable combinations, either fresh or frozen, can be substituted.

- Boneless chicken breast can be substituted for pork.

ORIENTAL FRUIT COMPOTE

**About 6 servings,
55 calories each**

This lightly glazed blend of fresh and canned fruit is as delicious as it is colorful. It makes a refreshing accompaniment or finish for any meal.

1 8-ounce can pineapple chunks in fruit juice

1 teaspoon cornstarch

2 medium-size oranges, peeled and sectioned

2 kiwifruit, peeled and thinly sliced

1. Drain pineapple juice into 1-cup microwave-safe measure. Blend in cornstarch.

2. MICROWAVE (high), uncovered, 1½–2 minutes or until mixture boils and thickens, stirring once. Set aside to cool.

3. Combine pineapple, oranges, and kiwifruit in serving bowl. Pour cooled sauce over fruit. Refrigerate if desired.

Rice and broccoli-topped ham slices are the interesting entree for this meal, which is finished off with warm apple muffins. Even when time is limited, you can still enjoy a warm, nutritious meal like this with only 275 calories. If desired, add a salad to complete the meal.

MENU
CALICO HAM SLICES
APPLE-BRAN MUFFINS

TIME GUIDE
About 30 minutes ahead:
Prepare Calico Ham Slices, steps 1 and 2.
Prepare Apple-Bran Muffins, steps 1 and 2.
Complete ham, steps 3–6.
Complete muffins, step 3.

CALICO HAM SLICES

**6 servings,
180 calories each**

Use one of the brands of lean or reduced-fat ham for this colorful combination. We've figured each slice as a serving, but the calories are low enough so you can easily enjoy 2 slices and still stay within most calorie limits.

¾ *cup water*

¾ *cup quick-cooking rice*

¼ *teaspoon salt*

1 *10-ounce package frozen chopped broccoli*

1 *2-ounce jar chopped pimiento, drained*

2 *tablespoons margarine*

2 *tablespoons flour*

1 *cup skim milk*

1½ *tablespoons lemon juice*

¼ *teaspoon salt*

¼ *teaspoon dry mustard*

6 *thin slices lean ham (about 12 ounces)*

1. MICROWAVE (high) water in covered 1-quart microwave-safe casserole 1½–2 minutes or until boiling. Add rice and salt; mix lightly. Place frozen broccoli and pimiento on rice. Cover with casserole lid.

2. MICROWAVE (high) 7–8 minutes or until water is absorbed. Let stand, covered, 5 minutes. While rice stands, combine margarine and flour in 2-cup microwave-safe measure.

3. MICROWAVE (high), uncovered, 30–45 seconds or until margarine is melted. Stir to combine; blend in milk.

4. MICROWAVE (high), uncovered, 2½–3 minutes or until mixture boils and thickens, stirring twice. Stir in lemon juice, salt, and mustard. Set aside.

5. Arrange ham slices on microwave-safe serving platter or baking dish. Cover with waxed paper.

6. MICROWAVE (high) 1½–2 minutes or until hot. Fluff rice with fork; spoon onto ham slices. Top with sauce.

APPLE-BRAN MUFFINS

**About 12 muffins,
95 calories each**

These nutritious muffins with bits of apple will appeal to the entire family.

⅔ cup skim milk

2 teaspoons vinegar

1 cup all-bran cereal

1 egg

2 tablespoons cooking oil

¼ cup sugar

½ cup unsifted all-purpose flour

¾ teaspoon ground cinnamon

½ teaspoon soda

1 apple, peeled and finely chopped

Toasted wheat germ, if desired

1. Combine milk and vinegar in 1-quart mixing bowl. Allow to stand a few minutes. Add cereal; allow to stand about 5 minutes or until milk is absorbed. Beat in egg and oil; stir in sugar. Mix in flour, cinnamon, and soda just until moistened. Fold in apple pieces.

2. Spoon batter into paper-lined microwave-safe muffin cups, filling cups ⅔ full. Sprinkle with wheat germ, if desired.

3. MICROWAVE (high) 6 muffins at a time, uncovered, 2–2½ minutes or until no longer doughy, rotating pan once. Repeat with remaining batter.

TIP

● Leftover batter can be covered tightly and refrigerated overnight. Increase microwave time to 2½–3 minutes.

This 305-calorie meal is great for late summer and fall since it uses many fresh produce items from this time of year. The leftover garlic sticks make great snacks to pack in lunch boxes.

MENU
ZUCCHINI-CHEESE CASSEROLE
TOASTED GARLIC STICKS

TIME GUIDE
About 30 minutes ahead:
Prepare Zucchini-Cheese Casserole.
Prepare Toasted Garlic Sticks.

ZUCCHINI-CHEESE CASSEROLE

**About 4 servings,
250 calories each**

Wondering what to do with all that zucchini from your garden? Here is a tasty recipe that is sure to please.

1½ *pounds zucchini, sliced
   (about 5 cups)*

1 *small onion, chopped*

1 *4-ounce can diced green
   chilies, drained*

3 *tablespoons flour*

½ *teaspoon salt*

⅛ *teaspoon pepper*

1 *cup (4 ounces) shredded
   cheddar cheese*

1 *egg*

1 *cup low-fat cottage cheese*

3 *tablespoons grated Parmesan
   cheese*

1. Combine zucchini and onion in 8- by 8-inch microwave-safe baking dish. Cover with waxed paper.

2. MICROWAVE (high) 10–12 minutes or until tender-crisp, stirring once. Add chilies, flour, salt, and pepper; mix well. Sprinkle with cheddar cheese. Beat together egg and cottage cheese; spoon over casserole, spreading evenly. Sprinkle with Parmesan cheese. Cover with waxed paper.

3. MICROWAVE (high) 6–8 minutes or until heated through (150° F), rotating dish once. Let stand, covered, 5–10 minutes.

TOASTED GARLIC STICKS

**12 sticks,
55 calories each**

Warm garlic sticks make the perfect accompaniment for many meals. Leftovers are good served as snacks another day.

1 tablespoon margarine

⅛ teaspoon parsley flakes

Dash garlic powder

6 7½-inch bread sticks

1. MICROWAVE (high) margarine in uncovered microwave-safe custard cup 30–45 seconds or until melted. Stir in parsley and garlic. Break each bread stick in half; brush with butter mixture. Arrange on paper plate.

2. MICROWAVE (high), uncovered, 45–60 seconds or until heated.

This delicious combination of zucchini soup and hot crabmeat sandwiches adds up to a nutritious lunch or light dinner for only 245 calories. They are ready to eat in just 20 minutes.

MENU
CREAMY ZUCCHINI SOUP
HOT CRABMEAT SANDWICHES

TIME GUIDE
About 20 minutes ahead:
Prepare Creamy Zucchini Soup, steps 1 and 2.
Prepare Hot Crabmeat Sandwiches, step 1.
Complete soup, step 3.
Complete sandwiches, step 2.

CREAMY ZUCCHINI SOUP

**About 4 servings,
45 calories each**

Serve steaming hot bowls of this flavorful soup often. It reheats well, so you may want to plan for leftovers to serve at another meal.

2 cups sliced zucchini (about 2 medium)

1 small onion, sliced

1 cup water

½ cup evaporated skim milk

2 teaspoons instant chicken bouillon

⅛ teaspoon dried basil leaves (optional)

Dash pepper

1. Combine zucchini, onion, and water in 1-quart microwave-safe casserole. Cover with casserole lid.

2. MICROWAVE (high) 7–8 minutes or until vegetables are tender, stirring once. Cool slightly. Pour into blender or food processor container. Process until smooth; combine with remaining ingredients in casserole. Cover.

3. MICROWAVE (high) 4–5 minutes or until hot, stirring once.

TIPS

- Skim milk can be substituted for evaporated skim milk; decrease the water to ¾ cup and increase the milk to ¾ cup.

- Try serving this soup chilled for a delightful summer cooler.

HOT CRABMEAT SANDWICHES

**4 sandwiches,
200 calories each**

English muffin halves, topped with crabmeat and cheese, make a delicious sandwich to serve anytime.

1 4-ounce package frozen crabmeat, thawed and drained

½ cup finely chopped celery

¼ cup shredded cheddar cheese

3 tablespoons mayonnaise

1 teaspoon snipped chives

½ teaspoon lemon juice

Dash garlic salt

2 English muffins, split and toasted

1 tomato, sliced thin

Parsley sprigs (optional)

1. Combine flaked crabmeat, celery, cheese, mayonnaise, chives, lemon juice, and garlic salt; mix well. Place muffins cut side up on microwave-safe serving plate. Top each muffin half with a tomato slice. Divide crab mixture among muffins; spread evenly.

2. MICROWAVE (high), uncovered, 1½–2 minutes or until filling is warm, rotating plate once. Garnish with parsley.

TIP

- Crab mixture can also be spread on 2 split croissants.

A cup of soup and a sandwich make a perfect lunch or light dinner. The soup uses frozen mixed vegetables to help make it especially quick. At only 305 calories, this combination is sure to be a winner.

MENU
QUICK VEGGIE SOUP
BACON-TOMATO SANDWICHES

TIME GUIDE
About 15 minutes ahead:
Prepare Quick Veggie Soup.
Prepare Bacon-Tomato Sandwiches.
Reheat soup if necessary.

QUICK VEGGIE SOUP

**About 4 servings,
60 calories each**

You won't believe how easy and good-tasting this soup is with only 4 ingredients!

*1 10-ounce package frozen
mixed vegetables*

1 14½-ounce can beef broth

⅛ teaspoon dried basil leaves

Dash pepper

1. Combine all ingredients in 1-quart microwave-safe casserole. Cover with casserole lid.
2. MICROWAVE (high) 10–12 minutes or until heated (150° F), stirring once.

TIP

● Cubed cooked beef or pork can be added in step 1 for a heartier soup; use about ½ cup. Calories will be higher.

BACON-TOMATO SANDWICHES

**4 servings,
245 calories each**

These colorful sandwiches are good served alone or with a cup of steaming hot soup.

*4 hamburger buns, split and
toasted*

*2 tablespoons mayonnaise or
salad dressing*

2 tablespoons plain yogurt

*8 slices Canadian bacon (about
8 ounces)*

1 medium tomato, sliced thin

½ cup alfalfa sprouts

1. Arrange buns cut side up on serving plate. Combine mayonnaise and yogurt; spread over cut side of buns. Set aside.
2. Place bacon around outside edges of microwave-safe serving plate. Cover with waxed paper.
3. MICROWAVE (high) 2–2½ minutes or until heated, rotating plate once. Top each bun half with a slice of bacon and tomato; top with sprouts.

CHAPTER
7
MAKE-AHEAD MEALS

Make-ahead meals are ideal for entertaining or for days when a busy schedule does not allow time to prepare the food before serving. They are for the cook who wants to make the food the night before or early in the day and simply pop it into the microwave to cook in the evening. The recipes are tasty enough for guests, but also ideal as downright good family fare, too.

Because the recipes are geared to entertaining, the servings are for six to eight or even ten to twelve. Most of the recipes can be halved easily if you want to enjoy the menus for smaller meals. Or you can use them for two meals, eating half when prepared and freezing half for later enjoyment. Remember that the cooking times will change if the recipe size is reduced or if the mixture is frozen.

Most of the entrees for the menus in this chapter are prepared ahead, refrigerated, and then cooked or heated at serving time. Many of the accompaniments are almost completely prepared and simply need to be set on the table or cut and served. The timings given for microwaving before serving are for refrigerator-temperature food. Be sure to shorten the time if the recipe was prepared only an hour or two ahead and left at room temperature. In the recipe "Tips," there are timings for those occasions when you want to serve the dish immediately.

The "Time Guides" include both the steps that should be done ahead and the amount of time necessary to complete the cooking at serving time. For the early preparation, we have listed just the various recipes and steps. But you can make even the early preparation less time-consuming by preparing part of one recipe while another cooks or stands.

Although a microwave time range is given in each recipe, the temperature probe can also be used in the final microwaving steps to determine doneness. If the food is cooked ahead and only needs reheating, the internal temperature of the food should reach about 150°F. Some meat items that are uncooked will require a higher temperature. A microwave thermometer can be used instead of the probe, or a conventional thermometer can be inserted after the food is removed from the microwave oven.

Recipes that can be stirred are perfect to make ahead and then reheat before serving. Soups, chowders, casseroles, and sauces are ideal to have in the refrigerator for busy days. Family members can quickly heat individual servings, or the entire dish can be heated. Some dishes even taste better prepared ahead since the flavors have longer to blend.

Marinated meats are ideal for make-ahead meals, too. Prepare them far enough in advance to obtain the desired flavor, as the longer they marinate, the stronger the flavor. When prepared an hour or two in advance, they can stand at room temperature. However, for longer marinating, they should be refrigerated. Plastic bags are ideal for marinating, since the juices can be held close to the food and turning the bag over is easy to do.

Refrigeration storage time is suggested in the recipes. This is the ideal length of time for quality and flavor to be at a peak. Most of the foods can be kept a day or two longer from a food safety standpoint, providing they have been properly cooled and refrigerated.

One advantage of make-ahead meals is that most of the preparation dishes are all washed and forgotten about by the time the food is served. This can really cut down on the cleanup following a company meal. Plan to use your microwave-safe serving dishes to eliminate any extra cooking dishes.

With these menus, you will be able to prepare meals at your leisure and still have valuable time to spend with your guests and family at serving time.

This make-ahead meal teams ground meat rolls with mashed potatoes and an aspic salad for just 440 calories. It can double as family and company fare. Since much of the preparation is done in advance, it is easy on the cook.

MENU
TOMATO ASPIC SALADS
FLORENTINE ROLLS
WHIPPED POTATOES

TIME GUIDE
Early in day or night before:
Prepare Florentine Rolls, steps 1–3.
Prepare Whipped Potatoes, steps 1 and 2.
Prepare Tomato Aspic Salads, steps 1 and 2.

About 25 minutes ahead:
Complete potatoes, step 3.
Complete rolls, steps 4 and 5.
Complete salads, step 3.
Reheat potatoes if necessary.

TOMATO ASPIC SALADS

**About 8 servings,
130 calories each**

No one will guess that fruit-flavored gelatin adds the delightful sweetness to this aspic.

2 14½-ounce cans stewed tomatoes, undrained

1 6-ounce package strawberry-flavored gelatin

2 stalks finely chopped celery

1 tablespoon vinegar

Spinach leaves

½ cup reduced-calorie buttermilk dressing

2 tablespoons finely chopped cucumber

1. Process tomatoes in food processor or blender container until smooth. Combine with gelatin in 4-cup microwave-safe measure; mix well.

2. MICROWAVE (high), uncovered, 4½–5 minutes or until mixture boils, stirring twice. Cool slightly. Stir in celery and vinegar. Oil eight ¾-cup molds; spoon mixture into molds. Cover and refrigerate until set, at least 3 hours.

3. *To Serve:* Unmold salads onto spinach. Mix together dressing and cucumber; spoon onto salads.

TIP

● Aspic can be chilled in a shallow pan and then cut into squares for serving.

FLORENTINE ROLLS

About 8 servings, 160 calories each

A spinach filling is swirled inside of this ground beef roll.

1 10-ounce package frozen chopped spinach

1 pound lean ground beef

1 8-ounce can pizza sauce

1 egg, beaten

¼ cup dry bread crumbs

2 tablespoons chopped onion

1 tablespoon parsley flakes

¼ teaspoon salt

¼ cup plain yogurt

2 tablespoons grated Parmesan cheese

1. MICROWAVE (high) spinach in package (remove foil if necessary) 4–5 minutes or until thawed. Squeeze out excess liquid; set aside.

2. Combine ground beef, ½ the pizza sauce, the egg, bread crumbs, onion, parsley, and salt; mix well. Place mixture on waxed paper. Flatten to rectangle 10 inches long and 8 inches wide. Set aside.

3. Mix spinach with yogurt and Parmesan cheese. Spread over meat mixture. Roll up jelly-roll fashion, starting with 10-inch side. Seal edges. Cut into 8 slices. Place cut side down on microwave meat rack. Cover and refrigerate up to 24 hours. Store remaining pizza sauce in covered container in refrigerator.

4. *To Serve:* Cover with waxed paper. MICROWAVE (high) 10–12 minutes or until meat is done (meat may still look pink but should be set). Spoon remaining pizza sauce over rolls.

5. MICROWAVE (high), uncovered, 1–2 minutes or until hot.

TIP

• To serve immediately, reduce time in step 4 to 6–7 minutes.

WHIPPED POTATOES

**About 8 servings,
150 calories each**

These mashed potatoes can be prepared a day ahead. Keep them in mind to ease preparation of holiday meals that include potatoes.

**6 medium potatoes, peeled and
  quartered (about 2½ pounds)**

¼ cup water

3 ounces Neufchâtel cheese

1 cup skim milk

1 tablespoon margarine

1 teaspoon snipped chives

½ teaspoon salt

¼ teaspoon garlic salt

Paprika

1. Combine potatoes and water in 2-quart microwave-safe casserole. Cover with casserole lid.

2. MICROWAVE (high) 14–16 minutes or until tender, stirring once. Drain. Cube cheese and add to potatoes along with skim milk, margarine, chives, and salts. Beat until potatoes are fluffy and light. Spread evenly in dish. Cover and refrigerate up to 24 hours.

3. *To Serve:* MICROWAVE (high), covered, 7–9 minutes or until heated through (150° F), stirring once. Sprinkle with paprika.

TIP

• To serve immediately, reduce time in step 3 to 3–4 minutes.

In this 235-calorie meal, turkey rolls and garden-fresh vegetables are microwaved to perfection. Serve it to family or guests.

MENU
TURKEY CORDON BLEU
FRESH VEGETABLE PLATTER

TIME GUIDE
Several hours ahead or night before:
Prepare Turkey Cordon Bleu, steps 1 and 2.
Prepare Fresh Vegetable Platter, step 1.

About 20 minutes ahead:
Prepare vegetables, step 2.
Complete turkey, step 3.
Complete vegetables, step 3, reheating if necessary.

TURKEY CORDON BLEU

**6 rolls,
190 calories each**

"Elegant but easy" describes this make-ahead fare.

6 slices turkey breast fillets (about 1 pound)

3 slices low-fat boiled ham (about 3 ounces)

3 slices Swiss cheese (about 2 ounces)

2 tablespoons dry bread crumbs

2 tablespoons grated Parmesan cheese

½ teaspoon paprika

1. Place turkey slices between sheets of plastic wrap. Pound with smooth side of meat mallet or rolling pin until ¼-inch thick. Top each fillet with ½ slice ham and ½ slice cheese, placing cheese at one end of fillet. Roll up jelly-roll fashion, starting with cheese end; secure with toothpick if necessary. Set aside.

2. Combine bread crumbs, Parmesan cheese, and paprika on waxed paper. Roll turkey rolls in crumb mixture. Place in 12- by 8-inch microwave-safe baking dish. Cover with plastic wrap and refrigerate up to 24 hours.

3. *To Serve:* Remove plastic wrap; cover with paper towel. MICROWAVE (high) 9–10 minutes or until turkey is done, rotating dish once.

TIP

- To serve immediately, decrease time in step 3 to 7–8 minutes.

FRESH VEGETABLE PLATTER

**About 6 servings,
45 calories each**

Attractive vegetable combinations can be assembled ahead for last-minute cooking.

2 cups cauliflower pieces

2 cups broccoli pieces

½ cup thinly sliced carrots

Water

1 tablespoon margarine

⅛ teaspoon dried tarragon
   leaves

⅛ teaspoon salt (optional)

1. Arrange cauliflower around outer edge of 9-inch microwave-safe serving plate. Next arrange a row of broccoli. Add carrots in center of plate. Sprinkle with a little water. Cover with plastic wrap and refrigerate up to 24 hours.

2. *To Serve:* MICROWAVE (high) 7–9 minutes or until vegetables are tender, rotating plate once. Let stand 5 minutes. Drain. Combine margarine, tarragon, and salt in 1-cup microwave-safe measure.

3. MICROWAVE (high) 30–45 seconds or until melted. Mix well and spoon over vegetables.

TIPS

- Other favorite seasonings can be substituted for tarragon.

- Frozen cut corn can be substituted for carrots.

- To retain the pretty green color, open the plastic wrap a little during the standing time in step 2.

This cool and refreshing 280-calorie menu is appealing when the weather is warm. Serve it for a special luncheon or supper. You are sure to enjoy the make-ahead preparation during carefree summer days.

MENU
CHICKEN-VEGETABLE RICE MOLD
PARMESAN ITALIAN BREAD

TIME GUIDE
Early in day or night before:
Prepare Chicken-Vegetable Rice Mold, steps 1–4.
Prepare Parmesan Italian Bread, steps 1 and 2.

About 10 minutes ahead:
Complete rice mold, step 5.
Complete bread, step 3.

CHICKEN-VEGETABLE RICE MOLD
About 6 servings, 145 calories each

This salad is a delicious blend of chicken chunks, summer vegetables, rice, and a lite Italian dressing. Serve it in a pretty bowl, or mold it and fill the center with fresh vegetables.

1 whole chicken breast, skinned and split (about 1 pound)
½ cup uncooked long-grain white rice
1 cup water
½ teaspoon salt
½ teaspoon cooking oil
1 cup chopped cucumber
1 medium tomato, chopped
½ cup chopped green pepper
¼ cup chopped radishes
¼ cup finely chopped carrot
½ cup reduced-calorie Italian salad dressing
Cucumber slices, cherry tomatoes, green pepper rings, or carrot curls (optional)

1. Place chicken breast skin side up in 8- by 8-inch microwave-safe baking dish. Cover with waxed paper.
2. MICROWAVE (high) 7–8 minutes or until done, rotating dish once. Cool. Remove bones; cut meat into bite-size pieces. Refrigerate.
3. Combine rice, water, salt, and oil in 1½-quart microwave-safe casserole. Cover with casserole lid.
4. MICROWAVE (high) 4–5 minutes or until mixture boils. Then MICROWAVE (low—30%) 10–11 minutes or until rice is tender and liquid absorbed. Uncover and cool. Add chicken and remaining ingredients except cucumber slices, cherry tomatoes, etc., to rice; toss lightly. Press into 5-cup mold or transfer to serving dish. Cover and refrigerate up to 24 hours.
5. *To Serve:* Invert mold onto serving plate. If desired, fill center with cucumber slices, cherry tomatoes, pepper rings, or carrot curls.

TIPS

- For best flavor, refrigerate salad at least 6 hours for flavors to blend. It will keep in the refrigerator for 2 to 3 days.

- If using leftover cooked chicken or turkey, use 2 cups.

- To use full power instead of the lower power setting in step 4, MICROWAVE 3 minutes and let stand 4 minutes, twice.

PARMESAN ITALIAN BREAD

About 9 servings, 135 calories each

Cheese, fresh herbs, and garlic add special flavor to this French bread.

1 small loaf French bread (about 8 ounces)

3 ounces Neufchâtel cheese

3 tablespoons grated Parmesan cheese

1 tablespoon snipped chives

1 tablespoon snipped parsley

⅛ teaspoon garlic powder

1. Cut bread in half lengthwise, cutting to, but not through, crust; set aside.

2. MICROWAVE (high) Neufchâtel cheese in uncovered 1-cup microwave-safe measure 30–45 seconds or until softened. Stir in remaining ingredients. Spread mixture on cut side of bottom piece of bread. Replace with top. Wrap in paper toweling. Place in plastic bag and refrigerate.

3. *To Serve:* Remove bread from plastic bag. MICROWAVE (high) 45–60 seconds or until bread feels warm.

Seafood in a sauce can be prepared ahead and reheated at another meal. A combination of wild and white rice finishes the meal with a total of just 240 calories. It's sure to please both guests and family.

MENU
SEAFOOD SUPREME
WHITE AND WILD RICE

TIME GUIDE
Early in day or night before:
Prepare Seafood Supreme, steps 1-4.
Prepare White and Wild Rice, steps 1-4.

About 20 minutes ahead:
Complete rice, step 5.
Complete seafood, step 5.
Reheat rice if necessary.

SEAFOOD SUPREME

About 6 servings, 125 calories each

Shrimp, scallops, and broccoli are cooked in a creamy wine sauce. Serve over rice or in individual shells.

1 cup water

1 clove garlic, minced

1 stalk celery, sliced

1 small onion, chopped

1 carrot, chopped

½ teaspoon salt

⅛ teaspoon pepper

1 teaspoon instant chicken bouillon

8 ounces frozen uncooked shrimp

8 ounces frozen uncooked scallops

4 cups broccoli pieces

¼ cup evaporated skim milk

¼ cup unsifted all-purpose flour

2 tablespoons dry white wine

1. Combine water, garlic, celery, onion, carrot, salt, pepper, and bouillon in 2-quart microwave-safe casserole. Cover with casserole lid.

2. MICROWAVE (high) 6–7 minutes or until vegetables are tender-crisp. Add shrimp, scallops, and broccoli. Cover.

3. MICROWAVE (high) 8–9 minutes or until scallops and shrimp are firm and translucent, stirring once. Combine milk and flour in 4-cup microwave-safe measure; mix well. Stir in juices from casserole.

4. MICROWAVE (high), uncovered, 3–4 minutes or until mixture boils and thickens, stirring once. Stir in wine. Pour over seafood. Cool, cover, and refrigerate up to 24 hours.

5. *To Serve:* MICROWAVE (high), covered, 9–11 minutes or until heated through (150° F), stirring once or twice.

TIPS

• If shrimp and scallops are not frozen, decrease time in step 3 to 6–7 minutes.

• To serve immediately, reduce microwave time in step 5 to 2–3 minutes.

WHITE AND WILD RICE

**About 6 servings,
115 calories each**

This seasoned blend of rice is a good accompaniment to many different entrees.

½ **cup uncooked wild rice**

1 **cup water**

1 **small onion, chopped**

1 **stalk celery, chopped**

½ **cup uncooked long-grain
white rice**

2 **teaspoons instant chicken
bouillon**

¼ **teaspoon salt**

¼ **teaspoon lemon pepper**

1 **cup water**

1. Combine wild rice and water in 1½-quart microwave-safe casserole. Cover with casserole lid.

2. MICROWAVE (high) 3–4 minutes or until mixture boils. Let stand, covered, at least 1 hour.

3. MICROWAVE (high) 4–5 minutes or until mixture boils vigorously. Add remaining ingredients. Cover.

4. MICROWAVE (high) 6–7 minutes or until mixture boils. Then MICROWAVE (low—30%) 15–17 minutes or until most of liquid is absorbed. Uncover and cool. Cover and refrigerate up to 48 hours.

5. *To Serve:* MICROWAVE (high), covered, 5–6 minutes or until heated through (150° F), fluffing with fork once.

TIPS

- When substituting black pepper for lemon pepper, reduce amount to ⅛ teaspoon.

- To serve immediately, omit step 5. Allow rice to stand about 5 minutes after cooking in step 4; fluff with fork and serve.

This menu centers around a Spanish classic. With make-ahead preparation, it takes only 20 minutes to serve. At just 260 calories, your guests will enjoy the meal as much as you do.

MENU
PAELLA
PITA TRIANGLES

TIME GUIDE
Several hours ahead or night before:
Prepare Paella, steps 1-5.
Prepare Pita Triangles, steps 1 and 2.

About 20 minutes ahead:
Complete paella, steps 6 and 7.
Complete triangles, step 3.

PAELLA

**About 6 servings,
230 calories each**

Zucchini adds color and lightness to this pretty Spanish main dish.

1 medium onion, chopped

1 clove garlic, minced

1 tablespoon water

⅔ cup uncooked long-grain white rice

1 16-ounce can tomatoes, undrained

2 cups shredded zucchini

3 tablespoons (¾ ounce) chopped pepperoni

1 2-ounce jar chopped pimiento, drained

1 teaspoon instant chicken bouillon

½ teaspoon salt

¼ teaspoon saffron

6 chicken drumsticks

Paprika

1 9-ounce package frozen artichoke hearts

1. Combine onion, garlic, and water in 2-quart microwave-safe casserole. Cover with casserole lid.

2. MICROWAVE (high) 3–4 minutes or until vegetables are just about tender, stirring once. Add rice and tomatoes. Cover.

3. MICROWAVE (high) 12–14 minutes or until rice is just about cooked. Add zucchini, pepperoni, pimiento, bouillon, salt, and saffron; mix lightly. Turn into shallow 1½- or 2-quart microwave-safe baking dish. Arrange drumsticks on rice. Sprinkle with paprika. Cover with plastic wrap or casserole lid.

4. MICROWAVE (high) 12–14 minutes or until chicken is done, rotating dish once. Set aside, covered.

5. MICROWAVE (high) artichokes in package (remove foil covering if necessary) 4–5 minutes or until tender. Arrange artichokes between chicken pieces. Cool. Cover with plastic wrap and refrigerate up to 24 hours.

3 ounces uncooked shrimp, peeled

6. *To Serve:* MICROWAVE (high), covered, 8–10 minutes or until edges are heated, rotating dish once. Let stand 5 minutes. Add shrimp; sprinkle with paprika.

7. MICROWAVE (high) 5–6 minutes or until heated through and shrimp are firm, rotating dish once.

TIPS

● Skin can be removed from chicken to reduce calories further.

● Other seafood such as clams or crab pieces can be substituted for shrimp.

● To serve immediately, add shrimp with artichokes. Omit cooking in step 6; MICROWAVE as directed in step 7.

PITA TRIANGLES

About 16 triangles, 15 calories each

Quick and easy bread triangles to accompany your favorite meal.

2 6-inch pita breads

1 tablespoon margarine

Dash garlic powder

1 teaspoon snipped parsley

1 tablespoon grated Parmesan cheese

Paprika

1. Cut through pita breads horizontally to form 4 rounds. Cut each round into quarters. Arrange on paper plate or paper towel–lined microwave-safe plate. Combine margarine, garlic, and parsley in microwave-safe custard cup.

2. MICROWAVE (high), uncovered, 30–45 seconds or until melted. Brush on each triangle. Sprinkle each with Parmesan cheese and paprika. Cover and refrigerate up to 24 hours.

3. MICROWAVE (high), uncovered, 1–1½ minutes or until heated.

TIP

● Other favorite seasonings can be added to margarine mixture.

Here is an interesting brunch or supper menu that features a quiche with a rice crust.

MENU
BROCCOLI-HAM QUICHE
MAKE-AHEAD OATMEAL MUFFINS

TIME GUIDE
Early in day or night before:
Prepare Broccoli-Ham Quiche, steps 1–3.
Prepare Make-Ahead Oatmeal Muffins, steps 1 and 2.

About 20 minutes ahead:
Complete quiche, step 4.
Complete muffins, step 3.

BROCCOLI-HAM QUICHE

**About 8 servings,
190 calories each**

Cooked rice makes the easy crust for this vegetable and ham quiche.

$1\frac{1}{2}$ **cups hot cooked rice**

1 egg, beaten

1 10-ounce package frozen chopped broccoli

2 eggs

8 ounces cubed cooked ham (about $1\frac{1}{3}$ cups)

$\frac{1}{2}$ **cup (2 ounces) shredded Swiss cheese**

1 tablespoon chopped pimiento

$\frac{1}{4}$ **teaspoon dry mustard**

1. Combine hot rice and 1 egg in 9-inch microwave-safe pie plate; mix well. Press mixture into bottom and up sides of plate to form a crust; set aside.

2. MICROWAVE (high) broccoli in package (remove foil wrap if necessary) 7–7½ minutes or until tender-crisp, turning package over once.

3. Combine 2 eggs, ham, cheese, pimiento, and mustard; mix well. Drain broccoli and add to mixture. Spoon into crust. Cool, cover with plastic wrap, and refrigerate up to 24 hours.

4. *To Serve:* MICROWAVE (high), covered, 5 minutes. Let stand 5 minutes. Rotate dish. Then MICROWAVE (medium—50%) 10–12 minutes or until center is just about set, rotating dish once. Let stand 5 minutes; cut into wedges.

TIPS

- To serve immediately, reduce time in step 4 to 3 minutes on high and 7–8 minutes on medium.

- To use full power instead of the lower power setting in step 4, MICROWAVE 3 minutes and let stand 3 minutes, twice.

MAKE-AHEAD OATMEAL MUFFINS

About 8 muffins, 140 calories each

These muffins have the old-fashioned goodness of buttermilk and rolled oats. You'll often want to have a batch in the refrigerator for quick cooking in the microwave.

1 egg
¼ cup packed brown sugar
¼ cup cooking oil
⅓ cup buttermilk or sour milk
½ cup unsifted all-purpose flour
¼ cup quick-cooking rolled oats
1 teaspoon baking powder
¼ teaspoon soda
¼ teaspoon salt

1. Beat egg; blend in sugar, oil, and buttermilk until smooth. Add remaining ingredients; stir just until moistened.

2. Spoon into paper-lined microwave muffin cups, filling half full. Cover and refrigerate up to 24 hours.

3. *To Serve:* MICROWAVE (high) 6 muffins at a time, uncovered, 2–2½ minutes or until no longer doughy, rotating pan once. For remaining 2 muffins, decrease time to 45–50 seconds.

TIPS

● When storing batter for longer than 24 hours, refrigerate it in a covered dish and then spoon into cups as needed.

● Batter can be sprinkled with toasted wheat germ or cinnamon sugar before cooking.

● When muffins are cooked immediately, decrease time to 1¾–2¼ minutes.

This 300-calorie meal will be a family favorite. Thanks to make-ahead preparation, it takes only 20 minutes on the day it is served. Extra peppers and salad make great "planned overs" for a quick meal or snack.

MENU
COLORFUL STUFFED PEPPERS
PINEAPPLE-ORANGE SQUARES

TIME GUIDE
Early in day or night before:
Prepare Colorful Stuffed Peppers, steps 1 and 2.
Prepare Pineapple-Orange Squares, steps 1-3.

About 20 minutes ahead:
Complete peppers, step 3.
Complete pineapple squares, step 4.

COLORFUL STUFFED PEPPERS

**8 servings,
185 calories each**

A mixture of ground beef, rice, and corn fills fresh green pepper shells.

4 medium green peppers
½ pound ground beef
½ pound ground turkey
1 egg
½ cup quick-cooking rice
½ teaspoon salt
⅛ teaspoon pepper
1 8-ounce can tomato sauce
½ cup frozen whole-kernel corn
4 tablespoons catsup

1. Cut peppers in half lengthwise; remove core and seeds. Place cut side up in 12- by 8-inch microwave-safe baking dish. Set aside.

2. Crumble ground beef and turkey into mixing bowl; mix in egg. Stir in remaining ingredients except catsup. Spoon mixture into peppers, mounding as necessary. Top each with ½ tablespoon catsup. Cover and refrigerate up to 24 hours.

3. *To Serve:* Cover peppers with waxed paper. MICROWAVE (high) 15–18 minutes or until meat is done (170° F), rotating dish once.

TIPS

● These peppers will be tender-crisp. For a softer texture, cover the peppers in step 1 and microwave 3–4 minutes or until hot. Drain juices from peppers and continue with step 2.

● Ground beef can be substituted for ground turkey.

● Peppers can be frozen up to 1 month after step 2. To heat, MICROWAVE (high) 20–25 minutes.

● To serve immediately, reduce time in step 3 to 13–15 minutes.

PINEAPPLE-ORANGE SQUARES

**About 12 servings,
115 calories each**

Fruit and cheese are blended in this easy gelatin salad. Children will enjoy helping with the preparation.

1 **15-ounce can crushed
   pineapple in fruit juice,
   undrained**

1 **3-ounce package orange-
   flavored gelatin**

2–3 **ice cubes**

1 **envelope whipped topping
   mix**

1 **11-ounce can mandarin
   oranges, drained**

1 **cup low-fat cottage cheese**

1. Pour pineapple with juice into 2-quart microwave-safe mixing bowl.

2. MICROWAVE (high), uncovered, 2–2½ minutes or until boiling. Stir in gelatin until dissolved. Add ice; stir until melted. Refrigerate until slightly thickened, about 1 hour.

3. Prepare topping mix as directed on package. Fold topping, oranges, and cottage cheese into gelatin mixture. Pour into 8- by 8-inch baking dish. Cover and refrigerate until set, about 2 hours or overnight.

4. Cut into squares and serve on lettuce, if desired.

TIP

● Other favorite flavors of gelatin and other fruit can be substituted.

This menu is perfect for entertaining on a warm summer evening. Since much of the preparation is done ahead, it leaves lots of time to spend with your guests. The foods will delight them, too, with only about 320 calories.

MENU
SLICED BEEF WITH MUSTARD SAUCE
CHUNKY POTATO SALAD

TIME GUIDE
Early in day or night before:
Prepare Sliced Beef with Mustard Sauce, steps 1–4.
Prepare Chunky Potato Salad.

About 15 minutes ahead:
Complete beef, step 5.

SLICED BEEF WITH MUSTARD SAUCE

**About 12 servings,
185 calories each**

This roast is cooked ahead, sliced thin, and served cold with a tasty mustard sauce. It is perfect for a summer buffet or picnic.

3-pound beef round tip roast

Liquid smoke

⅛ teaspoon garlic powder

1 teaspoon peppercorns, crushed

Mustard Sauce

⅓ cup plain yogurt

⅓ cup reduced-calorie sour cream

1 teaspoon prepared mustard

½–1 teaspoon Dijon mustard

¼ teaspoon dill weed

Sliced mushrooms and snipped chives or parsley for garnish (optional)

1. Sprinkle roast lightly with liquid smoke and garlic powder. Press crushed peppercorns into sides of roast. Place on microwave-safe meat rack. Cover with waxed paper.

2. MICROWAVE (high) 5 minutes. Then MICROWAVE (medium-high—70%) 10 minutes. Turn roast over; cover.

3. MICROWAVE (medium—50%) 10–15 minutes or until medium-rare (140° F). Uncover and cool. Cover and refrigerate up to 24 hours.

4. Combine yogurt, sour cream, mustards, and dill in small serving bowl; mix well. Cover and refrigerate up to 48 hours.

5. *To Serve:* Thinly slice meat and arrange on serving platter. If desired, garnish with sliced mushrooms and snipped chives or parsley. Serve with mustard sauce.

TIPS

• This meat is best cooked with a lower power setting.

• To crush peppercorns, place in plastic bag and pound with rolling pin.

CHUNKY POTATO SALAD

**About 8 servings,
135 calories each**

A lower-calorie cooked dressing and lots of vegetables make this summer classic lite and delicious.

6 medium potatoes, peeled and
  cut into chunks (about 4
  cups)

2 tablespoons water

2 tablespoons margarine

1 tablespoon flour

1 tablespoon sugar

½ teaspoon salt

½ teaspoon dry mustard

½ teaspoon dill weed

¼ cup water

3 tablespoons vinegar

1 egg, beaten

½ cup chopped celery

½ cup chopped zucchini or
  cucumber

¼ cup chopped radishes

2 green onions, chopped
  (including tops)

3 hard-cooked eggs, peeled and
  chopped

1. Combine potatoes and 2 tablespoons water in 2-quart microwave-safe casserole. Cover with casserole lid.

2. MICROWAVE (high) 11–13 minutes or until tender, stirring once. Drain and set aside.

3. MICROWAVE (high) margarine in uncovered 2-cup microwave-safe measure 30–45 seconds or until melted. Stir in flour, sugar, salt, mustard, dill, ¼ cup water, and vinegar.

4. MICROWAVE (high), uncovered, 1–1½ minutes or until mixture boils, stirring once. Stir in beaten egg, blending well.

5. MICROWAVE (high), uncovered, 30–45 seconds or until thickened, stirring once. Cool about 30 minutes.

6. Combine celery, zucchini, radishes, onions, and eggs with cooked potatoes; mix lightly. Add cooled dressing; mix just until combined. Cover and refrigerate up to 24 hours.

TIPS

- Allow salad to chill at least 3–4 hours for best flavor.

- If dressing or salad seems too thick, mix in 1–2 tablespoons skim milk.

What a combination—marinated beef, a salad of fresh vegetables, and a pretty vegetable side dish. The three recipes included here add up to just 370 calories. Most of the preparation is done the night before or early in the day. Then it takes minimal time and dishes to serve an attractive and delicious meal.

MENU
SKEWERED BEEF TERIYAKI
SPINACH SALAD
PEA PODS AND CARROTS

TIME GUIDE
Early in day or night before:
Prepare Skewered Beef Teriyaki, step 1.
Prepare Spinach Salad, steps 1-4.
Prepare Pea Pods and Carrots, step 1 and 2.

About 20 minutes ahead:
Complete pea pods, step 3.
Complete beef, steps 2 and 3.
Complete salad, step 5.

SKEWERED BEEF TERIYAKI

About 6 servings, 165 calories each

Simple preparation will make this an often-served family favorite.

1 **pound boneless top round steak, partially frozen**

3 **green onions, sliced (including tops)**

1 **clove garlic, minced**

¼ **cup soy sauce**

2 **tablespoons dry sherry**

1 **tablespoon honey**

1 **teaspoon sesame seed**

1 **teaspoon cooking oil**

⅛ **teaspoon ground ginger**

6 **10-inch wooden skewers**

1. Cut meat across grain into ¼-inch slices. Combine remaining ingredients. Pour over meat strips, coating evenly. Cover; refrigerate at least 3 hours or up to 24 hours, rearranging once or twice.

2. *To Serve:* Thread meat onto skewers. Place skewers across 8- by 8-inch microwave-safe baking dish. Brush with marinade.

3. MICROWAVE (high), uncovered, 5½–6 minutes or until done, rotating dish once and brushing with remaining marinade.

SPINACH SALAD

**About 6 servings,
150 calories each**

Make dressing several hours in advance to allow flavors to blend.

Dressing

¼ cup cooking oil

3 green onions, sliced (including tops)

2 tablespoons sugar

2 tablespoons white wine vinegar

2 tablespoons catsup

½ teaspoon Worcestershire sauce

¼ teaspoon salt

Salad

3 slices bacon

6 cups torn spinach leaves

2 cups (8 ounces) sliced fresh mushrooms

1 cup fresh bean sprouts

1. MICROWAVE (high) oil and onions in uncovered 2-cup microwave-safe measure 2½–3 minutes or until onions are tender, stirring once. Add sugar, vinegar, catsup, Worcestershire sauce, and salt. Mix or shake vigorously. Refrigerate at least 3 hours to allow flavors to blend.

2. Layer bacon between paper towels on paper plate.

3. MICROWAVE (high) 2½–3 minutes or until bacon is crisp. Crumble; set aside.

4. Toss spinach, mushrooms, and bean sprouts in serving bowl; cover and refrigerate up to 24 hours.

5. *To Serve:* Mix salad lightly with dressing. Sprinkle with bacon.

PEA PODS AND CARROTS

**About 6 servings,
55 calories each**

Glazed pea pods and carrots make an appealing combination.

2 cups diagonally sliced carrots

2 tablespoons water

3 ounces fresh pea pods (about 1 cup)

1 tablespoon margarine

1 tablespoon sliced almonds

1. Combine carrots and water in 1-quart microwave-safe casserole. Cover with casserole lid.

2. MICROWAVE (high) 6–7 minutes or until tender-crisp, stirring once. Uncover and cool. Cover and refrigerate up to 24 hours.

3. *To Serve:* Add pea pods. Cover and MICROWAVE (high) 4½–5 minutes or until pea pods are bright green. Drain. Add margarine; mix lightly. Sprinkle with almonds.

TIP

• To serve immediately, reduce time in step 3 to 2½–3 minutes.

This company menu combines a ham and noodle dish with carrots. It reheats beautifully and will make entertaining a breeze as well as keep you trim at only 375 calories.

MENU
HAY AND STRAW
SHERRIED CARROTS

TIME GUIDE
Early in day or night before:
Prepare Hay and Straw, steps 1–3.
Prepare Sherried Carrots, steps 1 and 2.

About 15 minutes ahead:
Complete pasta, step 4.
Complete carrots, step 3.

HAY AND STRAW

**About 5 servings,
315 calories each**

Two colors of pasta make this popular Italian dish look like a mixture of hay and straw. It is nice for making ahead or serving immediately. To speed the preparation, we cook the pasta conventionally while preparing the sauce in the microwave. However, the pasta cooks nicely in the microwave if you prefer that method.

4 ounces egg noodles (about 2 cups)

4 ounces spinach egg noodles (about 2 cups)

2 cups (8 ounces) sliced fresh mushrooms

1 clove garlic, minced

1 tablespoon margarine

12 ounces lean cooked ham, cubed (about 2½ cups)

½ cup evaporated skim milk

¼ teaspoon salt

¼ cup grated Parmesan cheese

1. Cook noodles as directed on package. Drain and rinse in cold water.

2. Combine mushrooms, garlic, and margarine in 2-quart microwave-safe casserole. Cover with casserole lid.

3. MICROWAVE (high) 3–3½ minutes or until mushrooms are just about tender. Add ham, milk, salt, Parmesan cheese, and cooked noodles; mix well. Cover and refrigerate up to 24 hours.

4. *To Serve:* MICROWAVE (high), covered, 10–12 minutes or until heated through (150° F), stirring once or twice.

TIPS

• To serve immediately, reduce microwave time in step 4 to 8–10 minutes.

• Cooked and drained Italian sausage can be substituted for ham.

SHERRIED CARROTS

**About 5 servings,
60 calories each**

Carrots require longer cooking than some vegetables, so they are often easier to serve if cooked ahead and then reheated. These have a delightful orange and sherry glaze.

4 cups sliced carrots (about 8 medium)

2 tablespoons water

½ tablespoon margarine

1 teaspoon sugar

1 tablespoon dry sherry

½ teaspoon grated orange peel

1. Combine carrots and water in 1-quart microwave-safe casserole. Cover with casserole lid.

2. MICROWAVE (high) 6–7 minutes or until tender-crisp, stirring twice. Let stand, covered, 5 minutes. Drain. Stir in remaining ingredients. Cool, cover, and refrigerate up to 24 hours.

3. *To Serve:* MICROWAVE (high), covered, 4–5 minutes or until heated through, stirring once.

TIP

- To serve immediately, decrease time in step 3 to 1½–2 minutes.

Manicotti is always a favorite but is known for being time-consuming to make. This recipe has two pluses—first, it is assembled in advance of serving; second, the noodles are not precooked, so you save a step and the uncooked noodles are much easier to fill. To complete this menu of 390 calories we offer a colorful marinated vegetable salad.

MENU
MAKE-AHEAD MANICOTTI
MARINATED VEGETABLE MEDLEY

TIME GUIDE
Several hours ahead or night before:
Prepare Make-Ahead Manicotti, steps 1–3.
Prepare Marinated Vegetable Medley.

About 45 minutes ahead:
Complete manicotti, steps 4 and 5.

MAKE-AHEAD MANICOTTI

About 8 servings, 320 calories each

No need to cook manicotti shells ahead as they can cook right in the sauce. You'll appreciate the ease of preparation, and your family will enjoy the good taste.

1 16-ounce can tomatoes, undrained

1 15-ounce can tomato sauce

2 tablespoons chopped green pepper

1 teaspoon sugar

½ teaspoon Italian seasoning

⅛ teaspoon garlic powder

1 15-ounce carton ricotta cheese (about 2 cups)

½ cup grated Parmesan cheese

1 4-ounce can sliced mushrooms, drained

2 eggs

1 8-ounce package manicotti shells

¾ cup water

1 cup (4 ounces) shredded mozzarella cheese

1. Cut tomatoes into quarters and combine tomatoes, sauce, green pepper, sugar, seasoning, and garlic powder in 1½-quart microwave-safe casserole. Cover with casserole lid.

2. MICROWAVE (high) 6–8 minutes or until mixture boils, stirring once. Set aside.

3. Combine ricotta cheese, Parmesan cheese, mushrooms, and eggs; mix well. Stuff mixture into uncooked manicotti shells. Arrange shells in 12- by 8-inch microwave-safe baking dish. Pour tomato mixture over shells, making sure that all are covered with sauce. Cover with plastic wrap and refrigerate up to 24 hours.

4. *To Serve:* MICROWAVE (high), covered, 15 minutes. Rotate dish. Add water. Cover. Then MICROWAVE (medium—50%) 16–18 minutes or until noodles are tender, rotating dish once. Sprinkle with mozzarella cheese.

5. MICROWAVE (high), uncovered, 2–3 minutes or until cheese is melted. Let stand about 10 minutes before serving.

TIP

● To use full power instead of the lower power setting in step 4, MICROWAVE 3 minutes and let stand 3 minutes, 3 times.

MARINATED VEGETABLE MEDLEY

About 8 servings, 70 calories each

Marinated vegetables are always great for make-ahead meals. These have a lite buttermilk dressing.

3 cups cauliflower pieces (1 small head)

2 cups (8 ounces) sliced fresh mushrooms

2 tablespoons water

3 cups broccoli pieces (1 bunch)

3 green onions, sliced

½ cup reduced-calorie buttermilk dressing

2 tablespoons sunflower seeds

¼ teaspoon water

1. Combine cauliflower, mushrooms, and water in 2-quart microwave-safe mixing bowl. Cover with plastic wrap.

2. MICROWAVE (high) 2½–3 minutes or until tender-crisp. Drain and rinse in cold water. Add broccoli, onions, and dressing; mix lightly. Set aside.

3. Combine sunflower seeds and ¼ teaspoon water in 1-cup microwave-safe measure.

4. MICROWAVE (high), uncovered, 4½–5½ minutes or until lightly toasted, stirring 3 or 4 times. Sprinkle seeds over salad. Cover and refrigerate at least 12 hours. Mix lightly before serving.

TIP

● Other favorite salad dressing can be substituted.

CHAPTER
8
FREEZER MEALS

Today, with more women as well as men employed outside the home, a common mealtime dilemma is, "What can I serve for dinner tonight?" The freezer can work hand in hand with the microwave oven to provide convenient, nutritious meals quickly on busy nights, solving this problem. On occasions when there is more time to cook, such as on a weekend, you can make several dishes, freeze them, and heat when time is at a premium. For even more convenience, make a double batch, eat one now, and freeze the other for later. During peak produce times, be sure to freeze extra quantities of recipes using seasonal fruits and vegetables.

In this chapter we provide some recipes for individual and family-size portions. Package foods in serving sizes that accommodate your family's needs. To save on freezer space and containers, freeze individual items on baking sheets. When frozen firm, they can be placed in freezer bags. If you line casserole dishes with plastic wrap, aluminum foil, or freezer paper before adding the food, you can remove the food, once frozen, wrap it, and freeze. When ready to reheat, just remove the wrap and return the food to the original dish. Take advantage of freezer containers and bags designed for microwave use. This will eliminate the need to transfer frozen foods to new containers for heating.

Be sure to select suitable containers for freezing. They should not allow air to reach the food since this robs the food of flavor and quality. It is also important to have a cold enough temperature. Foods should be stored at 0°F or lower for maximum quality. Frequent opening of the freezer door causes a rise in temperature. The freezer compartment on refrigerators is not usually recommended for extended storage of frozen foods.

Suggested storage times are given with each recipe. This will help you to serve the food while it is still at peak quality. However, if the wrap or temperature has not been adequate, the quality will deteriorate sooner. After this recommended storage time, the food will still be usable, but the quality may not be as good.

When you plan to use a temperature probe to heat the food, insert a straw into the food before freezing. This space allows the probe to be inserted while the food is still frozen. The area where the probe is inserted often heats more quickly than other areas, so be sure to reinsert the probe once or twice to assure that the entire dish is the desired temperature. Most casseroles are best heated to a temperature of about 150°F.

Label each package with contents, number of servings, date, and cookbook page for heating instructions. For convenience, make a checklist of foods in the freezer with dates and recommended storage times.

The "Time Guides" in this chapter include only the timing for heating the foods from the freezer. Many are for complete meals that can come from the freezer. Use the individual heating times when you want to make your own recipe combinations.

Smaller quantities, like individual servings, reheat well from the frozen state. Larger quantities reheat quite well when they can be stirred. Dishes that are not stirred require long, slow heating to warm the center without overheating the edges. With some of these dishes, it may be more convenient to allow the mixture to thaw in the refrigerator for about 24 hours. This usually cuts the heating time to about half that needed for the frozen food.

If your microwave oven has an auto-defrost feature, you can use it to thaw frozen foods. Just keep in mind that they are programmed to thaw very gradually and that it will take longer than the timings we have given. Check your oven manufacturer's instructions for information and guidelines on using this feature.

Team your freezer with the microwave oven and you won't have a problem about what to serve for a meal. When someone asks the question "What are you making for dinner tonight?" you can answer, "It's in the freezer and ready to heat."

FREEZER MEATBALLS

Prepare and freeze these meatballs; then turn them into three different meals. You can use your own imagination, too, adding them to some of your own favorite sauces and casseroles. This recipe makes about 36 meatballs, 60 calories each.

2 pounds lean ground beef

½ cup chopped onion

½ cup dry bread crumbs

½ cup skim milk

2 eggs

1 tablespoon snipped parsley

1 teaspoon seasoned salt

1 teaspoon paprika

¼ teaspoon pepper

1. Combine all ingredients; mix well. Shape into about 36 meatballs, 1¼ inches in diameter. Place half of meatballs in 12- by 8-inch microwave-safe baking dish.

2. MICROWAVE (high) 6–7 minutes or until meat is set, rearranging once if necessary. Drain; set aside. Repeat with remaining meatballs. Cool and package about 12 meatballs in each of 3 freezer containers. Label and freeze up to 3 months.

MENU
MEATBALL STROGANOFF

MEATBALL STROGANOFF

About 4 servings, 375 calories each

Here is a lite version of a family favorite. Serve it over rice for a delicious hearty meal of 375 calories.

2 cups (8 ounces) sliced fresh mushrooms

2 tablespoons dry onion soup mix

1 tablespoon water

12 Freezer Meatballs (see recipe above)

2 tablespoons flour

1 cup water

½ teaspoon prepared mustard

⅓ cup plain yogurt

1 teaspoon parsley flakes

2 cups rice, prepared

1. Combine mushrooms, soup mix, and water in 2-quart microwave-safe casserole. Cover with casserole lid.

2. MICROWAVE (high) 2–3 minutes or until mushrooms are tender. Add meatballs. Blend together flour, water, and mustard; stir into meatballs. Cover.

3. MICROWAVE (high) 10–12 minutes or until meatballs are hot, stirring twice. Stir in yogurt and parsley.

4. Prepare rice on stove. Serve with stroganoff.

MENU
MEATBALLS WITH SPAGHETTI SAUCE

MEATBALLS WITH SPAGHETTI SAUCE

About 4 servings, 450 calories each

Here is an easy-to-make, great-tasting sauce that is just right for frozen meatballs. When served with 1 ounce of cooked spaghetti, the calories will be about 450.

⅓ cup chopped onion

1 clove garlic, minced

1 16-ounce can tomatoes, undrained

1 6-ounce can tomato paste

¼ cup water

1 teaspoon sugar

½ teaspoon salt

⅛ teaspoon pepper

¼ teaspoon dried oregano leaves

¼ teaspoon dried basil leaves

1 bay leaf

12 Freezer Meatballs (see recipe on page 177)

4 ounces spaghetti, prepared

1. Combine onion and garlic in 2-quart microwave-safe casserole. Cover with casserole lid.

2. MICROWAVE (high) 2–3 minutes or until partially cooked. Add remaining ingredients. Cover.

3. MICROWAVE (high) 15–18 minutes or until meatballs and sauce are heated through.

4. Prepare spaghetti. Serve with meatball mixture.

MENU
MEATBALLS BOURGUIGNON

MEATBALLS BOURGUIGNON

**About 4 servings,
375 calories each**

Use meatballs from the freezer for this delicious and quick 375 calorie entree. Serve in soup bowls, along with French bread to dip in the delicious sauce.

3 medium carrots

1 cup water

1 tablespoon instant beef bouillon

1 clove garlic, minced

1 bay leaf

2 tablespoons flour

3 tablespoons dry red wine

12 Freezer Meatballs (see recipe on page 177)

1 4.5-ounce jar whole mushrooms, drained

1 14-ounce jar small whole onions, drained

1 teaspoon dried parsley flakes

4 slices French bread

TIP

● If onions are large, cut in half.

1. Halve carrots lengthwise; cut into 1-inch pieces. Combine with water, bouillon, garlic, and bay leaf in 2-quart microwave-safe casserole. Cover with casserole lid.

2. MICROWAVE (high) 7–8 minutes or until carrots are partially cooked. Mix together flour and wine; stir into carrot mixture. Add remaining ingredients; cover.

3. MICROWAVE (high) 10–12 minutes or until mixture boils and thickens, stirring twice. Serve with French bread.

Have the makings for breakfast in the freezer. You can make up the muffinwiches anytime. Enjoy some immediately and freeze the remainder for another meal. A great in-the-freezer breakfast for only 240 calories.

MENU
SCRAMBLED MUFFINWICHES
CRANBERRY FIZZ

TIME GUIDE
About 5 minutes ahead:
Prepare Cranberry Fizz, step 3.
Prepare Scrambled Muffinwiches, steps 7 and 8.

SCRAMBLED MUFFINWICHES

**6 muffinwiches,
180 calories each**

Scrambled eggs and crumbled bacon top English muffins for a delicious breakfast on the go.

 3 *slices bacon*

 4 *eggs*

 3 *tablespoons water*

 ¼ *teaspoon salt*

 1 *cup (4 ounces) sliced fresh mushrooms*

 1 *tablespoon margarine*

1½ *tablespoons flour*

 ½ *cup skim milk*

 ¼ *cup shredded cheddar cheese*

 3 *English muffins, split*

Snipped fresh chives (optional)

1. Layer bacon between paper towels on microwave-safe pie plate.
2. MICROWAVE (high) 2½–3 minutes or until bacon is crisp. Set aside.
3. Beat together eggs, water, and salt in 2-cup microwave-safe measure.
4. MICROWAVE (high), uncovered, 3–3½ minutes or until just about set, stirring twice. Set aside. Combine mushrooms and margarine in 2-cup microwave-safe measure.
5. MICROWAVE (high), uncovered, 2–2½ minutes or until mushrooms are tender. Remove mushrooms with slotted spoon; add to eggs. Blend flour into liquid. Stir in milk.
6. MICROWAVE (high), uncovered, 2–2½ minutes or until mixture boils and thickens, stirring once. Stir in cheese until melted. Gently stir in eggs. Cool. Divide mixture between muffin halves, spreading evenly. Crumble bacon and sprinkle on top along with chives. Freeze on baking sheet. When frozen, wrap, label, and freeze up to 1 month.
7. *To Serve:* Unwrap desired number of muffinwiches. Wrap each in paper toweling.
8. MICROWAVE (high) one muffin at a time 1–1¼ minutes or until warm. Let stand about 2 minutes. Then MICROWAVE (high) 20–30 seconds or until hot.

CRANBERRY FIZZ

**42 cubes,
20 calories each**

Keep these frozen cubes in plastic freezer bags for a refreshing drink any time of day.

2 cups water

¼ cup sugar

3 bags green tea

1 medium orange, sliced

12 cloves

2 cinnamon sticks

1 quart cranberry juice cocktail

**Favorite diet lemon-lime or
ginger ale beverage**

1. Combine water, sugar, tea bags, orange slices, cloves, and cinnamon in 2-quart microwave-safe mixing bowl.

2. MICROWAVE (high), uncovered, 8–10 minutes or until boiling, stirring once or twice. Let stand 5 minutes. Remove tea bags, orange slices, and spices. Add cranberry juice cocktail. Pour into 3 ice cube trays. Freeze until firm. Remove from trays and place in freezer bag. Label and freeze up to 3 months.

3. *To Serve:* Place 3 cubes in each glass; fill glass with favorite beverage. Or place cubes in blender or food processor container. Add 1 cup beverage for each 6 cubes. Process until slushy. Pour into glasses, filling ⅔ full. Fill with remaining beverage.

TIP

- Black tea can be substituted for green; color will be slightly darker.

Coleslaw and ham sandwiches are always favorites. You will love the convenience of having these ready in the freezer for a quick meal of only 215 calories. The coleslaw makes a nice addition to many other meals, so you will want to make up a lot of it when cabbage is plentiful.

MENU
HAM 'N' SWISS ON RYE
FREEZER COLESLAW

TIME GUIDE
About 10 minutes ahead:
Prepare Freezer Coleslaw, step 5.
Prepare Ham 'n' Swiss on Rye, step 3.

HAM 'N' SWISS ON RYE

**12 sandwiches,
175 calories each**

Here's a good way to use up leftover ham. Keep a supply of these sandwiches on hand in the freezer for quick meals or snacks.

**8 ounces lean ham, cut into
  pieces**
**6 ounces Swiss cheese, cut into
  pieces**
⅓ cup margarine
1 tablespoon snipped chives
1 tablespoon prepared mustard
1 teaspoon poppy seed
6 rye hamburger buns, split

1. Process ham and cheese in food processor container until mixture is in fine particles. Set aside. Combine margarine, chives, mustard, and poppy seed in 1-cup microwave-safe measure.

2. MICROWAVE (high), uncovered, 45–60 seconds or until margarine is melted. Pour over ham mixture; process until blended. Divide mixture among halves of buns, spreading evenly. Place on baking sheet and freeze until firm. Package in freezer bag, label, and freeze up to 1 month.

3. *To Serve:* Wrap buns individually in paper toweling. MICROWAVE (high) one bun at a time 45–60 seconds or until filling is warm.

TIPS

- If food processor is not available, finely chop ham and shred Swiss cheese. Mix with fork in mixing bowl.

- Other favorite buns can be substituted.

FREEZER COLESLAW

**About 14 servings,
40 calories each**

This flavorful coleslaw is easy to prepare and makes a colorful addition to any meal. You will love the convenience of having it ready in the freezer.

1 teaspoon salt

1 medium head cabbage (about 1½ pounds)

¼ cup water

¼ cup vinegar

¼ cup sugar

¼ teaspoon celery seed

¼ teaspoon dry mustard

Dash pepper

1 medium carrot, shredded

⅓ cup finely chopped green pepper

1 tablespoon finely chopped onion

1. Sprinkle salt over cabbage in large mixing bowl; let stand about 1 hour. Squeeze out liquid.

2. Combine water, vinegar, sugar, celery seed, mustard, and pepper in 2-cup microwave-safe measure.

3. MICROWAVE (high), uncovered, 1½–2 minutes or until mixture boils. Stir; then MICROWAVE (high) 1 minute longer to blend flavors. Cool.

4. Add carrot, green pepper, and onion to cabbage. Add cooled dressing; mix well. Pack into 3 freezer containers. Cover, label, and freeze up to 3 months.

5. *To Serve:* MICROWAVE (high) one uncovered container at a time 2–2½ minutes or until edges are slightly warm. Break up with fork and allow to finish defrosting at room temperature for about 5 minutes.

TIPS

● Other favorite coleslaw vegetables such as celery or radishes can be added or substituted for the carrot and green pepper.

● Coleslaw can be frozen in larger or smaller portions. Just increase or decrease the microwave time in step 5 proportionately.

Children will love "parents' night out" when you have these freeze-ahead sandwiches ready for them to reheat. The pizzas and salads add up to only a 295-calorie meal. They also make great late-evening snacks.

MENU
FRENCH BREAD PIZZAS
FROZEN MINI FRUIT SALADS

TIME GUIDE
About 5 minutes ahead:
Remove Frozen Mini Fruit Salads from freezer.
Prepare French Bread Pizzas, steps 4 and 5.

FRENCH BREAD PIZZAS

**About 12 servings,
225 calories each**

These individual sandwich pizzas are great to have on hand for a quick meal or snack. Just heat 'n' eat!

1 pound lean ground beef

¼ cup chopped onion

1 16-ounce can pizza sauce

¼ cup sliced green olives

¼ cup (1 ounce) diced pepperoni

1 16-ounce loaf French bread

1½ cups (6 ounces) shredded mozzarella cheese

1. Crumble ground beef into 1-quart microwave-safe casserole. Add onion.

2. MICROWAVE (high), uncovered, 5–6 minutes or until no longer pink, stirring once. Drain. Stir in sauce, olives, and pepperoni. Set aside.

3. Cut bread in half lengthwise, then cut each half into 6 equal pieces. Spread each piece with about ¼ cup meat mixture. Top each with about 2 tablespoons cheese. Place on baking sheet; freeze until firm. Package in freezer bag, label, and freeze up to 1 month.

4. *To Serve:* Place 4 sandwiches at a time on microwave-safe plate. Cover with paper towel.

5. MICROWAVE (high) 4–5 minutes or until meat is warm and cheese begins to melt, rotating plate once.

TIPS

• Meat mixture can also be spread on hamburger buns.

• Ground turkey can be substituted for half or all of ground beef.

• For 1 sandwich, MICROWAVE 1½–2 minutes. For 2 sandwiches, MICROWAVE 2½–3 minutes.

• Other favorite pizza ingredients can be substituted for pepperoni and green olives.

FROZEN MINI FRUIT SALADS

About 18 salads, 70 calories each

These easy, refreshing salads can also be served as desserts.

1 15¼-ounce can crushed pineapple in fruit juice

¼ cup sugar

1 tablespoon cornstarch

1 egg, beaten

1 8-ounce package Neufchâtel cheese

1 17-ounce can chunk-style mixed fruit, drained

1 medium-size ripe banana, mashed

¼ cup chopped maraschino cherries with juice

1. Drain pineapple juice into 4-cup microwave-safe measure. Mix in sugar, cornstarch, and egg.

2. MICROWAVE (high), uncovered, 2–3 minutes or until mixture boils and thickens, stirring once. Cool.

3. MICROWAVE (high) cheese in uncovered mixing bowl 30–40 seconds or until softened. Mix until creamy; add pineapple, mixed fruit, banana, and cherries. Fold in cooled pudding mixture. Line 18 muffin cups with paper liners. Spoon mixture into cups, filling about three-quarters full. Freeze until firm. Remove from cups and package in freezer bag. Label and freeze up to 1 month. Remove papers from salads and let stand at room temperature about 10 minutes before serving.

4. *To Serve:* Remove papers from salads and let stand at room temperature about 10 minutes.

TIP

● Salad can also be frozen in a 1- to 1½-quart mold. Allow to stand at room temperature about 20 minutes before unmolding and serving.

Tacos are known for being somewhat messy to eat. This variation is eaten with a spoon or fork, eliminating that problem. The meat mixture is made ahead and frozen and then combined with tortilla chips, lettuce, tomato, and cheese for a quick supper or lunch. Frozen vegetables are always convenient to have on hand for meal accompaniments. The combination of tacos and green beans adds up to a slenderizing 330 calories.

MENU
MEXICAN SPOON TACOS
FRENCH-CUT GREEN BEANS

TIME GUIDE
About 20 minutes ahead:
Prepare Mexican Spoon Tacos, step 3.
Prepare French-Cut Green Beans, steps 1 and 2.
Complete tacos, steps 4 and 5.
Complete beans, step 3.

MEXICAN SPOON TACOS

**About 6 servings,
280 calories each**

In this version of tacos, the meat is spooned over tortilla chips instead of into taco shells. You'll enjoy the ease of eating these as well as the quick preparation from the freezer.

1 pound lean ground beef

¼ cup chopped onion

1 10-ounce can tomatoes with green chilies, undrained

½ teaspoon garlic salt

½ teaspoon ground cumin

½ teaspoon chili powder

⅛ teaspoon pepper

2 teaspoons cornstarch

2 cups tortilla chips

1 small tomato, chopped

1½ cups shredded lettuce

⅓ cup shredded Monterey Jack cheese

1. Crumble ground beef into 1-quart microwave-safe casserole; add onion.

2. MICROWAVE (high), uncovered, 5–6 minutes or until no longer pink, stirring once. Drain; stir to break meat into pieces. Mix in tomatoes, garlic salt, cumin, chili powder, and pepper. Cool, cover, label, and freeze up to 2 months.

3. *To Serve:* MICROWAVE (high) meat mixture, covered, 5–6 minutes or until mixture is thawed, stirring once. Stir in cornstarch.

4. MICROWAVE (high), uncovered, 7–8 minutes or until mixture boils and thickens, stirring once or twice.

5. Arrange tortilla chips on 6 plates. Spoon hot meat mixture onto chips. Top with tomato, lettuce, and cheese.

TIP

● If tomatoes with green chilies are not available, use regular tomatoes and add about 2 tablespoons chopped green chilies.

FRENCH-CUT GREEN BEANS

**About 6 servings,
50 calories each**

Vegetables from the freezer are always quick to prepare in the microwave.

**2 10-ounce packages frozen
French-cut green beans**

**1 6-ounce can water chestnuts,
drained and sliced**

¼ teaspoon salt

1 tablespoon margarine

1. Place beans in 2-quart microwave-safe casserole. Cover with casserole lid.

2. MICROWAVE (high) 10–12 minutes or until just about done, stirring once. Mix in water chestnuts, salt, and margarine. Cover.

3. MICROWAVE (high) 2–3 minutes or until heated through.

Meat and potatoes can be combined in a lite menu if the fat is kept to a minimum and servings are not too generous. This menu features items from the freezer for only 265 calories.

MENU
PEPPER STEAK
CREAMY POTATO PUFFS

TIME GUIDE
About 25 minutes ahead:
Prepare Pepper Steak, step 3.
Prepare Creamy Potato Puffs, step 3.
Complete steak, steps 4 and 5.

PEPPER STEAK

**About 5 servings,
205 calories each**

Your family is sure to enjoy the delicious flavor of this entree. Prepare it when there is time for slow simmering to tenderize the meat; then heat it right from the freezer when your time is at a premium.

1 pound beef round tip steak, cut into $\frac{1}{8}$-inch strips

2 green onions, chopped

1 clove garlic, minced

2 tablespoons soy sauce

1 teaspoon grated fresh gingerroot

1 teaspoon instant beef bouillon

1 medium green pepper, cut into chunks

1 cup (4 ounces) sliced fresh mushrooms

1 tablespoon cornstarch

1 medium tomato, cut into eighths

1. Combine beef, onions, garlic, soy sauce, ginger, and bouillon in 2-quart microwave-safe casserole. Let stand 1 hour or refrigerate overnight. Cover with casserole lid.

2. MICROWAVE (high) 5–6 minutes or until boiling. Then MICROWAVE (low—30%) 15 minutes, stirring once. Stir in green pepper and mushrooms. Cover and MICROWAVE (low—30%) 15–20 minutes or until meat is tender, stirring once. Cool. Cover tightly, label, and freeze up to 3 months.

3. *To Serve:* Loosen lid slightly. MICROWAVE (high) 9–10 minutes or until warm, rearranging once. Mix in cornstarch. Cover loosely.

4. MICROWAVE (high) 4–5 minutes or until mixture boils and thickens, stirring once. Stir in tomato.

5. MICROWAVE (high), uncovered, 1–2 minutes or until tomato is heated.

TIPS

- To use full power instead of the lower power setting in step 2, MICROWAVE 3 minutes and let stand 4 minutes, 5 times.

- About $\frac{1}{8}$ teaspoon ground ginger can be substituted for gingerroot.

CREAMY POTATO PUFFS

**About 12 servings,
60 calories each**

Here is a good potato recipe to have in the freezer for easy entertaining or to add a special touch to family meals. For a really professional touch, pipe the mixture from a pastry bag, using a star tip.

4–5 medium potatoes (about 1½ pounds)

2 tablespoons water

3 ounces Neufchâtel cheese

2 tablespoons grated Parmesan cheese

⅓ cup skim milk

½ teaspoon onion salt

Dash pepper

1 egg

1 teaspoon dried parsley flakes

1. Combine potatoes and water in 1½-quart microwave-safe casserole. Cover with casserole lid.

2. MICROWAVE (high) 10–12 minutes or until tender, stirring once. Mash potatoes; blend in Neufchâtel and Parmesan cheeses, milk, onion salt, and pepper. Beat in egg. Spoon mixture into 12 mounds on waxed paper–covered baking sheet. Sprinkle with parsley. Freeze about 3 hours or until firm. Transfer puffs to freezer bag or container. Close tightly, label, and freeze up to 2 weeks.

3. *To Serve:* Place 5 puffs on microwave-safe serving plate. Cover with waxed paper. MICROWAVE (high) 5–6 minutes or until heated through, rotating plate once.

TIP

● To heat all of the puffs, place 6 at a time on microwave-safe serving plate. Cover with waxed paper and MICROWAVE (high) 5½–6½ minutes. Repeat with remaining puffs.

How nice to come home after a busy day and have a meal ready to microwave and eat. All you need to do is set the table and prepare a salad. This meal is sure to be a family favorite, and it has only 350 calories.

MENU
SWISS STEAK
FREEZER TWICE-BAKED POTATOES

TIME GUIDE
About 25 minutes ahead:
Prepare Swiss Steak, step 3.
Prepare Freezer Twice-Baked Potatoes, steps 4 and 5.
Complete steak, step 4.

SWISS STEAK

**About 4 servings,
275 calories each**

Swiss steak requires slow cooking to tenderize. Once cooked, the meat can be frozen for a quick microwaved meal.

1 pound beef round steak, cut ½ inch thick

Natural beef browning and seasoning powder

1 tablespoon flour

1 medium carrot, sliced thin

1 medium onion, sliced thin

1 16-ounce can tomatoes, undrained

1 tablespoon brown sugar

1 tablespoon Worcestershire sauce

¼ teaspoon dried oregano leaves

¼ teaspoon pepper

1. Cut meat into 4 serving pieces. Sprinkle with browning powder; coat with flour. Pound on both sides with meat mallet to tenderize. Place meat in oven-cooking bag; set in 12- by 8-inch microwave-safe baking dish. Add remaining ingredients to bag. Secure bag with nylon tie or string. Cut six ½-inch slits in top of bag.

2. MICROWAVE (high) 5 minutes or until mixture boils. Then MICROWAVE (low—30%) 45–60 minutes or until meat is tender, rearranging meat once. Open bag and cool. Wrap, label, and freeze up to 3 months.

3. *To Serve:* MICROWAVE (high), covered, 7–8 minutes or until edges are heated. Let stand about 5 minutes.

4. MICROWAVE (high) 5–6 minutes or until heated through.

TIPS

● To heat individual servings, MICROWAVE in step 3 for 4–5 minutes, rearranging once.

● If browning powder is omitted, brown meat in skillet before microwaving.

● Meat can be reheated in step 3 at medium-high (70%) power for 18–20 minutes; omit standing time.

FREEZER TWICE-BAKED POTATOES

**About 8 servings,
75 calories each**

*What a convenience to have a supply of these potatoes in the freezer. Use them as a
quick meal accompaniment or just heat one or two for a quick snack.*

4 large baking potatoes

½ cup skim milk

¼ cup plain yogurt

**2 tablespoons grated Parmesan
cheese**

1 teaspoon snipped chives

½ teaspoon salt

Dash pepper

¼ cup shredded cheddar cheese

Paprika

1. Scrub potatoes; pierce each once or twice with fork.

2. MICROWAVE (high) 12–14 minutes or until potatoes are just about tender, turning and rearranging potatoes once. Cool enough to handle.

3. Cut potatoes in half lengthwise; scoop insides into bowl, leaving about ¼ inch potato in shell. Mash potato well. Blend in milk, yogurt, Parmesan cheese, chives, salt, and pepper; beat until light. Spoon potato mixture back into shells, mounding mixture as necessary. Top each with cheddar cheese; sprinkle with paprika. Wrap, label, and freeze up to 3 months.

4. *To Serve:* Place 4 frozen potato halves, spoke-fashion, on microwave-safe serving plate. Cover with waxed paper.

5. MICROWAVE (high) 6–7 minutes or until heated through, rotating plate once.

TIPS

- For 1 or 2 potato halves, MICROWAVE 2–3 minutes.

- For ease in storing, freeze potatoes on baking sheet. Once they are frozen, transfer potatoes to a freezer bag. Close tightly and freeze. Then just remove the desired number of potatoes as needed.

This 375-calorie menu, featuring lamb, goes from freezer to table in 15 minutes. You can use the same idea for patties made from lean ground beef as well. Enjoy the rice cups with other entrees. You will like the convenience of having them ready in the freezer.

MENU
MINTED LAMB PATTIES
VEGETABLE-RICE CUPS

TIME GUIDE
About 15 minutes ahead:
Prepare Minted Lamb Patties, steps 2 and 3.
Prepare Vegetable-Rice Cups, steps 4 and 5.
Complete lamb patties, steps 4 and 5.

MINTED LAMB PATTIES

**4 patties,
295 calories each**

A quick and easy mint sauce adds the special touch to these lamb patties that can be cooked right from the freezer.

1 pound ground lamb

1 egg, slightly beaten

¼ cup quick-cooking rolled oats

1 tablespoon instant minced onion

½ teaspoon seasoned salt

¼ teaspoon dried tarragon leaves

⅛ teaspoon pepper

Natural meat browning and seasoning powder

½ tablespoon apple jelly

¼ teaspoon dried mint leaves

1. Combine all ingredients except browning powder, jelly, and mint; mix lightly. Shape into 4 patties. Sprinkle lightly with browning and seasoning powder. Stack patties for freezing, placing a double layer of waxed paper between patties. Wrap, label, and freeze for up to 2 months.

2. *To Serve:* Unwrap patties and place on microwave-safe meat rack. Cover with waxed paper.

3. MICROWAVE (high) 7–8 minutes or until just about done, rotating dish once. Let stand 5 minutes. Combine jelly and mint in 1-cup microwave-safe measure.

4. MICROWAVE (high), uncovered, 30–45 seconds or until bubbly. Spoon or brush sauce over patties. Cover.

5. MICROWAVE (high) 2–3 minutes or until meat is done.

TIPS

● To cook one patty, MICROWAVE 2–2½ minutes. Brush with sauce and MICROWAVE 30–60 seconds or until done.

- For two patties, MICROWAVE 4–5 minutes. Brush with sauce and MICROWAVE 1–1½ minutes or until done.

- Jelly and mint can be frozen along with patties. Just place in plastic wrap and tuck into package. Then transfer to cup when ready to heat.

VEGETABLE-RICE CUPS

**18 servings,
80 calories each**

Since a larger quantity of rice takes about as long to cook as a small batch, we have made this recipe large enough to use for several meals. You may want to serve some immediately and freeze the remainder for later use.

4 cups hot water

2 cups uncooked long-grain white rice

½ cup finely chopped fresh broccoli

½ cup chopped fresh mushrooms

¼ cup finely chopped celery

¼ cup finely chopped carrot

2 green onions, chopped

1 teaspoon salt

1. Combine water and rice in 2-quart microwave-safe casserole. Cover with casserole lid.

2. MICROWAVE (high) 8–10 minutes or until mixture boils. Add remaining ingredients. Cover.

3. MICROWAVE (medium—50%) 14–16 minutes or until water is just about absorbed. Fluff with fork. Let stand, covered, 5 minutes. Uncover and cool. Divide mixture among 18 paper-lined muffin cups, pressing rice into cups. Freeze until firm. Then package in freezer bag, label, and freeze up to 1 month.

4. *To Serve:* Place 4 cups on microwave-safe plate. Cover with waxed paper.

5. MICROWAVE (high) 3½–4½ minutes or until heated through, rotating plate once. Invert and remove papers.

TIPS

- To heat 1 cup, MICROWAVE 45–60 seconds. For 2 cups, MICROWAVE 1½–2 minutes.

- Once the rice is pressed into the cups, the cups can be transferred to a baking sheet and frozen until firm. This is helpful if you do not have enough muffin cups.

- Double paper liners make it easier to remove and handle the cups.

- To use full power instead of the lower power setting in step 3, MICROWAVE 4 minutes and let stand 4 minutes, twice.

No need to stop for Chinese take-out food when you have this meal in the freezer. Complete the pork while you enjoy the soup as the first course. Served with ½ cup rice, the meal adds up to about 435 calories.

MENU
WONTON SOUP
SWEET AND SOUR PORK

TIME GUIDE
About 30 minutes ahead:
Prepare Wonton Soup, steps, 3–5.
Prepare Sweet and Sour Pork, step 3.
Serve soup while completing pork, step 4.

WONTON SOUP

**About 6 servings,
115 calories each**

Chicken-filled wontons are made ahead, frozen, and added to broth as needed. This is a good accompaniment for Oriental or stir-fried dishes. Note that the recipe makes about 24 wontons, but only 12 are used in the recipe, so you have extras to use for another meal.

8 ounces skinned and boned chicken breast, cut into pieces

¼ cup sliced water chestnuts

1 tablespoon soy sauce

1 tablespoon dry white wine or sherry

½ teaspoon sugar

24–30 wonton wrappers

2 14½-ounce cans chicken broth

1½ tablespoons soy sauce

1 green onion, sliced thin (including top)

1. Process chicken and water chestnuts in food processor container until in fine pieces. Add 1 tablespoon soy sauce, wine, and sugar; process until blended.

2. Place 1 wonton wrapper at a time in palm of hand with point toward you. Place scant teaspoon of filling just below center of wrapper. Moisten top edges of wrapper with water. Fold in half; press edges to seal. Moisten corners; overlap at center and press to seal. Repeat with remaining filling and wrappers. Place on waxed paper–lined baking sheet. Freeze until firm. Package in freezer bag, label, and freeze up to 1 month.

3. *To Serve:* Combine broth, 1½ tablespoons soy sauce, and green onion in 1½-quart microwave-safe casserole. Cover with casserole lid.

4. MICROWAVE (high) 7–8 minutes or until steaming hot; add 12 wontons. Cover.

5. MICROWAVE (high) 8–9 minutes or until wontons are tender, stirring once or twice.

TIPS

• To remove fat from chicken broth, refrigerate until fat solidifies. Lift off fat with fork before combining with other ingredients in step 3.

- Instant chicken bouillon and water can be substituted for chicken broth. Use 4 teaspoons bouillon and 3½ cups water. Calories will be slightly lower.

- You can use about 3½ cups of your own homemade chicken broth, too.

- Thinly sliced Chinese cabbage, fresh mushrooms, or pea pods can be added to soup along with wontons.

- If you don't have a food processor, finely chop the chicken and water chestnuts. The chicken will be easier to chop when partially frozen.

SWEET AND SOUR PORK

About 6 servings, 220 calories each

This Chinese favorite freezes well. Green pepper is added halfway through the heating time to prevent overcooking. For convenience, just freeze the pepper in a small plastic bag and tape it to the pork dish.

1 cup thinly sliced carrot

1 tablespoon water

2 cups cubed cooked lean pork (about 10 ounces)

1 8-ounce can pineapple chunks in fruit juice, undrained

¼ cup sugar

¼ cup vinegar

¼ cup catsup

1 teaspoon instant chicken bouillon

1½ tablespoons cornstarch

1 medium green pepper, cut into 1-inch pieces

1 medium tomato, cut into wedges

1. Combine carrot and water in 1-cup microwave-safe measure. Cover with plastic wrap.

2. MICROWAVE (high) 2–3 minutes or until tender-crisp. Combine carrot, pork, pineapple, sugar, vinegar, catsup, and bouillon in 1½-quart microwave-safe freezer container. Cover, label, and freeze up to 3 months.

3. *To Serve:* MICROWAVE (high), covered, 5–6 minutes or until thawed, stirring once. Stir in cornstarch and green pepper.

4. MICROWAVE (high), uncovered, 7–8 minutes or until mixture boils and thickens, stirring once or twice. Gently stir in tomato. If desired, serve each portion with ½ cup rice.

TIP

- The completed recipe can also be frozen in single-serving quantities. To heat, MICROWAVE 4–5 minutes, stirring once.

Keep these dishes in the freezer for a quick 415-calorie supper. When chicken is frozen shortly after cooking, it does not develop a "leftover" taste.

MENU
CHEESY BROCCOLI CHICKEN
FLUFFY WHITE RICE

TIME GUIDE
About 20 minutes ahead:
Prepare Cheesy Broccoli Chicken, step 7.
Prepare Fluffy White Rice, step 4.
Complete chicken, step 8.

CHEESY BROCCOLI CHICKEN

About 5 servings, 275 calories each

A light cheese sauce enhances this favorite chicken and broccoli dish.

1 whole chicken breast, skinned and split (about 16 ounces

1 10-ounce package frozen chopped broccoli

1 tablespoon margarine

1 tablespoon flour

¾ cup skim milk

½ cup (2 ounces) shredded cheddar cheese

2 tablespoons mayonnaise

¼ teaspoon salt

2 slices bread

1 tablespoon margarine

2 tablespoons grated Parmesan cheese

1. Place chicken breast in 8- by 8-inch square microwave-safe baking dish. Cover with plastic wrap.

2. MICROWAVE (high) 6–7 minutes or until done. Remove chicken to cool; discard juices.

3. MICROWAVE (high) broccoli in package (remove foil outerwrap if necessary) 5–6 minutes or until tender. Open package and set aside.

4. MICROWAVE (high) 1 tablespoon margarine and flour in uncovered 2-cup microwave-safe measure 30–45 seconds or until margarine is melted. Stir until smooth. Blend in milk.

5. MICROWAVE (high), uncovered, 2½–3 minutes or until mixture boils and thickens, stirring once. Add cheese; stir until melted. Blend in mayonnaise and salt.

6. Cut chicken into pieces, removing bones; return to same 8- by 8-inch square microwave baking dish. Top with broccoli and cheese sauce. Spread bread with 1 tablespoon margarine; cut into ½-inch cubes. Place on chicken. Sprinkle with Parmesan cheese. Cool, cover, label, and freeze up to 3 months.

7. *To Serve:* Cover dish with waxed paper. MICROWAVE (high) 10 minutes. Let stand 5 minutes. Rotate dish.

8. Then MICROWAVE (high) 5–7 minutes or until center is hot.

TIPS

- About 2 cups leftover cubed cooked chicken can be substituted for chicken breast.

- To heat casserole without freezing, prepare through step 6, except for freezing. Cover with waxed paper and MICROWAVE (high) 8–10 minutes or until heated through, rotating dish once.

FLUFFY WHITE RICE

About 5 servings, 140 calories each

Serve this recipe immediately or freeze for a quick future meal accompaniment.

1 cup uncooked long-grain rice

2 cups water

1 teaspoon salt

1 teaspoon cooking oil

1. Combine all ingredients in 1½-quart microwave-safe casserole. Cover with casserole lid.

2. MICROWAVE (high) 6–7 minutes or until mixture boils. Let stand 10 minutes.

3. MICROWAVE (high) 5–6 minutes or until liquid is just about absorbed. Let stand 5 minutes. Fluff with fork. Uncover and cool. Package in 1½-pint freezer container.

4. *To Serve:* MICROWAVE (high), covered, 3–4 minutes or until hot, stirring once.

This menu includes a creamed chicken mixture that can be served alone or varied by serving it over rice, pasta, or vegetables. If either the vegetables or rice are frozen, just thaw the chicken mixture about two-thirds of the way and then heat or cook the vegetable or rice while the chicken stands. Complete the heating of the chicken just before serving. The menu has about 300 calories.

MENU
CHICKEN A LA KING
EASY BROCCOLI

TIME GUIDE
About 25 minutes ahead:
Prepare Chicken à la King, step 5.
Prepare Easy Broccoli.
Reheat chicken if necessary.

CHICKEN A LA KING

**About 4 servings,
255 calories each**

This versatile dish is traditionally served over toast points or rice. For change of pace, try it over cooked broccoli or asparagus spears!

**1 cup (4 ounces) sliced fresh
   mushrooms**

½ cup chopped celery

¼ cup chopped red pepper

**2 tablespoons finely chopped
   onion**

2 tablespoons margarine

2 tablespoons flour

1 cup skim milk

**2 teaspoons instant chicken
   bouillon**

¼ teaspoon salt

⅛ teaspoon dried thyme leaves

5–6 drops hot pepper sauce

2 cups cubed cooked chicken

**1 10-ounce package frozen
   peas and carrots**

1. Combine mushrooms, celery, red pepper, onion, and margarine in 2-quart microwave-safe mixing bowl.

2. MICROWAVE (high), uncovered, 3–4 minutes or until vegetables are tender. Drain juices into 2-cup microwave-safe measure. Blend in flour. Stir in milk.

3. MICROWAVE (high), uncovered, 2½–3 minutes or until mixture boils and thickens, stirring once. Stir in bouillon, salt, thyme, and pepper sauce. Pour over vegetables. Cool. Stir in chicken. Set aside.

4. MICROWAVE (high) peas and carrots in package (remove foil if necessary) 3½–4 minutes or until thawed. Stir into chicken mixture. Divide mixture evenly between two 3-cup microwave-safe freezer containers. Cover, label, and freeze up to 3 months.

5. *To Serve:* MICROWAVE (high) one container at a time 8–10 minutes or until hot, stirring or rearranging once or twice.

TIP

● When mixture is frozen in one container, increase microwave time in step 5 to 13–15 minutes or until hot, stirring 2 or 3 times.

EASY BROCCOLI

**About 4 servings,
45 calories each**

Serve this simple recipe as a base for creamed sauces or as an accompaniment for poultry or beef.

*1 10-ounce package frozen
broccoli spears*

1 tablespoon margarine

⅛ teaspoon tarragon leaves

⅛ teaspoon seasoned salt

1. Place broccoli in 1-quart microwave-safe casserole. Cover with casserole lid.

2. MICROWAVE (high) 5–6 minutes or until just about tender, rearranging pieces once. Drain. Add margarine, tarragon, and salt. Cover.

3. MICROWAVE (high) 1–2 minutes or until broccoli is tender. Stir lightly to coat evenly.

Here is a nice menu for summer. Use it as a lunch or light supper. The calories total only 360. Both the recipes in this menu are very versatile and can be used as snacks or part of another meal.

MENU
STUFFED PITA POCKETS
MARINATED VEGETABLES

TIME GUIDE
About 10 minutes ahead:
Prepare Marinated Vegetables, step 4.
Prepare Stuffed Pita Pockets, step 4.

STUFFED PITA POCKETS

**8 pita pockets,
220 calories each**

Individual sandwiches are always good to have on hand in the freezer. Pita bread reheats nicely in the microwave because it is less likely to overheat than some other types of bread.

1 pound ground turkey

⅛ teaspoon fennel seed

1 8-ounce can tomato sauce

¼ cup sliced ripe olives

1 tablespoon grated Parmesan cheese

¼ teaspoon sugar

¼ teaspoon dried basil leaves

¼ teaspoon dried oregano leaves

⅛ teaspoon garlic powder

1 cup (4 ounces) shredded mozzarella cheese

8 4-inch pita breads

1. Crumble turkey into 1-quart microwave-safe casserole. Add fennel; cover with casserole lid.

2. MICROWAVE (high) 5–6 minutes or until no longer pink. Drain. Add tomato sauce, olives, Parmesan cheese, sugar, basil, oregano, and garlic powder.

3. MICROWAVE (high), uncovered, 2–3 minutes or until mixture is hot. Cool. Stir in mozzarella cheese. Carefully cut edge of bread rounds with scissors to open up on one side. Divide mixture among rounds. Place on baking sheet. Freeze until solid. Package in freezer bag, label, and freeze up to 3 months.

4. *To Serve:* Wrap 2 pocket breads individually in paper towels. MICROWAVE (high) 1½ minutes. Let stand 2 minutes. Then MICROWAVE (high) 1–1½ minutes or until hot.

TIPS

● If desired, use half lean ground beef and half ground turkey. Calories will be slightly higher.

● To heat one pita bread, decrease timings in step 4 to 45 seconds and 45–60 seconds.

MARINATED VEGETABLES

**About 4 cups,
140 calories each**

*Keep a supply of these tasty marinated vegetables in the freezer for a quick
accompaniment to any meal.*

**1 16-ounce package frozen
combination vegetables
(broccoli, carrots, water
chestnuts, red peppers)**

**1 cup (4 ounces) sliced fresh
mushrooms**

¼ cup water

¼ cup vinegar

2 tablespoons sugar

2 tablespoons cooking oil

½ teaspoon celery seed

½ teaspoon garlic salt

¼ teaspoon dry mustard

¼ teaspoon paprika

¼ teaspoon dried oregano leaves

1. Combine vegetables and mushrooms in 1½-quart microwave-safe casserole. Cover with casserole lid.

2. MICROWAVE (high) 7–8 minutes or until vegetables are tender-crisp, stirring once. Set aside to cool. Combine remaining ingredients in 1-cup microwave-safe measure.

3. MICROWAVE (high), uncovered, 2–2½ minutes or until mixture boils and flavors are blended. Pour over vegetables; mix well. Cool and refrigerate overnight. Pack desired quantity in freezer containers. Cover, label, and freeze up to 3 months.

4. *To Serve:* Place contents in microwave-safe serving dish. MICROWAVE (high), uncovered, 2–2½ minutes or until defrosted, stirring twice.

TIPS

● Mixture can also be defrosted in refrigerator overnight or at room temperature for a couple of hours.

● Other favorite vegetable combinations, either frozen or fresh, can be substituted.

TV DINNER TIPS

Prepare your own TV dinners and package in microwaveable plastic or paperboard trays. We've included one idea here, but you can create your own favorite combinations, too. For the best use of your time, prepare the meal and enjoy part of it immediately and plan to freeze the remainder in individual dinners.

TV dinners are easiest to prepare by just cooking extras and then packaging the leftovers on dinner trays for freezing. A variety of combinations freeze and heat well in the microwave. Occasionally, special preparation is needed to assure that all foods heat evenly and properly. In the menu below, the rice tended to dry out before the other foods were hot, so we added a little water just before heating. If using mashed potatoes, you may want to arrange them with an indentation in the center since they are often slow to reheat. Sliced meat is best spread out or rolled up so it is not in one large mass. If you do prepare a dinner and find that one part is heated before another portion, just remove the heated part and continue to cook the remainder for a short period.

This menu makes six TV dinners of 405 calories each.

MENU
CHICKEN KIEV
RICE PILAF
VEGETABLE COMBINATION

TIME GUIDE
Up to 1 month ahead:
Prepare TV Dinner, step 1-3.

About 10 minutes ahead:
Prepare TV Dinner, step 4.

1. Prepare Rice Pilaf recipe as directed. Place ½ cup in small compartment of microwave-safe dinner tray.

2. Prepare Chicken Kiev as directed. Add one roll to each tray. Spoon any remaining butter sauce over each roll.

3. Add ½ cup of your favorite brand of frozen vegetable combination (carrots, cauliflower, broccoli) to each tray. Wrap tightly, label, and freeze up to 1 month.

4. *To Serve:* Unwrap desired number of trays. Add 1 tablespoon water to rice on each tray. Cover each with waxed paper. MICROWAVE (high) one dinner at a time 5-6 minutes or until foods are heated, rotating plate once. Let stand 1-2 minutes before serving.

CHICKEN KIEV

**6 servings,
235 calories each**

Chicken Kiev is unbelievably easy to do in the microwave. Whether you prepare it for immediate enjoyment or freeze for later use, it is sure to be a favorite.

3 tablespoons margarine

3 tablespoons dry bread crumbs

3 tablespoons grated Parmesan cheese

½ teaspoon paprika

3 whole boneless chicken breasts, skinned and halved (about 21 ounces)

Salt and pepper

6 teaspoons snipped chives

1. Cut margarine into 6 even stick-shaped pieces. Place in freezer. Combine bread crumbs, Parmesan cheese, and paprika; set aside.

2. Place each chicken breast half between sheets of plastic wrap. Pound with smooth side of meat mallet or rolling pin until ¼ inch thick. Sprinkle each piece with salt and pepper and 1 teaspoon chives. Place 1 stick margarine on each piece. Tuck in sides and fold over ends to form roll. Press to seal chicken surfaces together.

3. Roll each in crumb mixture, coating well. Place in 9-inch microwave-safe pie plate. Refrigerate at least 30 minutes to chill. Cover with paper towel.

4. MICROWAVE (high) 12–15 minutes or until chicken is done, rotating dish twice.

RICE PILAF

**6 servings,
120 calories each**

This is such a nice flavor combination, you will want to serve it often.

1 cup long-grain white rice

2 cups water

1 teaspoon instant chicken bouillon

1 teaspoon margarine

½ teaspoon salt

2 tablespoons snipped parsley

1 green onion, chopped (including top)

1. Combine all ingredients in 1-quart microwave-safe casserole. Cover with casserole lid.

2. MICROWAVE (high) 5–6 minutes or until mixture boils. Then MICROWAVE (low—30%) 12–14 minutes or until water is absorbed. Fluff with fork.

TIPS

- To use full power instead of the lower power setting in step 2, MICROWAVE 3 minutes and let stand 4 minutes.

- 1 tablespoon snipped chives can be substituted for the green onion.

9
DESSERTS

Dessert is often the high point of a meal, so you will be pleased to discover that it can also be a part of lite dining. The recipes in this chapter include eggs, dairy products, and fruit, making them nutritious additions to your meals rather than just "empty" calories.

You will find desserts as basic as cobblers and custards or as elegant as fancy frozen creations and airy soufflés. There is a dessert here to accompany most any menu. Included are make-ahead desserts, those from the freezer, the quick and easy, as well as desserts for one or two, family meals, and those you would serve when entertaining guests. Some snack dessert ideas are included in the Mini-Meals chapter.

Any of the menus in this book will allow for the additional calories of dessert. The recipes range from 50 to 165 calories. When planning your meals, try to balance a menu that is a little higher in calories with a lower calorie finale, like one of the fruit desserts. If your meal is very low in calories, feel free to splurge on one of the higher calorie sweets, like pie or cake. Also, try to contrast color, flavor, texture, and temperature of foods when selecting the dessert creation to complete a meal.

You will discover that many of the desserts can be made ahead or prepared in the early part of the menu, leaving the microwave free for cooking the entree and other accompaniments.

So, save room for dessert and try some of the delicious guilt-free selections in this chapter. You will find many sweet endings here.

PEARS WITH RASPBERRY SAUCE

**About 4 servings,
105 calories each**

This refreshing raspberry sauce is also good served over canned pears or peaches.

**2 ripe fresh pears, peeled,
halved, and cored**

⅓ cup water

**½ 10-ounce package (about ½
cup) frozen sweetened
raspberries, water thawed**

1 tablespoon honey

1 teaspoon cornstarch

Dash ground cinnamon

Sliced almonds (optional)

1. Combine pears and ⅓ cup water in 1-quart microwave-safe casserole. Cover with casserole lid.

2. MICROWAVE (high) 3–4 minutes or until pears are tender. Uncover and set aside.

3. Process raspberries in blender or food processor container until smooth. Pour into 2-cup microwave-safe measure. Add water to make ⅔ cup. Stir in honey, cornstarch, and cinnamon.

4. MICROWAVE (high), uncovered, 1½–2½ minutes or until mixture boils and thickens, stirring once. Cool.

5. To serve, place drained pears in 4 sherbet glasses or individual dishes. Top with raspberry sauce. Garnish with almond slices.

TIPS

● Bartlett pears are best for cooking.

● To prevent browning, place peeled pears in water that contains 1 tablespoon lemon juice.

● Pears can turn brown after cooking if not fully ripe.

LEMON-SAUCED KIWIFRUIT AND STRAWBERRIES

**About 4 servings,
115 calories each**

This light lemon sauce makes a refreshing topping for many favorite fruits.

½ cup water

¼ cup sugar

2 teaspoons cornstarch

1 tablespoon margarine

1 teaspoon lemon juice

**1 kiwifruit, peeled and sliced
thin**

1 cup sliced fresh strawberries

1. Combine water, sugar, and cornstarch in 2-cup microwave-safe measure; stir to dissolve sugar.

2. MICROWAVE (high), uncovered, 2–2½ minutes or until mixture boils and thickens slightly, stirring once. Stir in margarine and lemon juice. Set aside.

3. Divide kiwifruit and strawberries among 4 individual dishes. Serve topped with sauce.

CARAMEL FLAN

**4 servings,
130 calories each**

Light, yet sweet, this flan makes a nice dessert following a spicy meal.

3 tablespoons sugar

3 tablespoons water

1¼ cups skim milk

2 eggs

2 tablespoons sugar

⅛ teaspoon salt

1 teaspoon vanilla

1. Combine 3 tablespoons sugar and water in 1-cup microwave-safe measure. Stir well.
2. MICROWAVE (high), uncovered, 4½–6½ minutes or until lightly browned. Pour slowly, in thin stream, onto a buttered cookie sheet. Set aside.
3. MICROWAVE (high) milk in uncovered 2-cup microwave-safe measure 2½–3½ minutes or until hot, but not boiling. Combine eggs, 2 tablespoons sugar, salt, and vanilla in a small mixing bowl; beat well. Slowly blend egg mixture into hot milk.
4. MICROWAVE (high), uncovered, 1–1½ minutes or until mixture begins to thicken around edge stirring once.
5. Break carmelized sugar into small pieces or crush with a rolling pin. Divide half of caramelized sugar among four 5-ounce custard cups. Divide custard mixture among cups.
6. MICROWAVE (medium—50%), uncovered, 1½–2½ minutes or until just about set, rearranging once. Cool.
7. To serve, invert custards onto dessert plates and garnish with remaining caramelized sugar.

CREAMY ALMOND CUSTARD

**About 4 servings,
125 calories each**

A light combination of custard and a topping of almonds makes an easy dessert.

1⅓ cups skim milk

2 eggs, well beaten

3 tablespoons sugar

½ teaspoon almond extract

1 tablespoon sliced almonds

1. Combine milk, eggs, sugar, and extract; mix well. Pour into four 5-ounce microwave-safe custard cups.
2. MICROWAVE (high), uncovered, 5–6 minutes or until just about set, rearranging once. Sprinkle each with sliced almonds. Serve warm or cold.

CHOCOLATE-ALMOND SOUFFLE

About 4 servings, 165 calories each

Two favorite flavors blend together in this lite dessert that is suitable for a family meal or guests.

¾ **cup skim milk**

2 **teaspoons unflavored gelatin**

¼ **cup semisweet chocolate pieces**

1 **teaspoon vanilla**

¼ **teaspoon almond extract**

1 **envelope whipped topping mix, prepared**

Sliced almonds (optional)

1. Combine milk and gelatin in 2-cup microwave-safe measure.
2. MICROWAVE (high), uncovered, 1½–2½ minutes or until gelatin is dissolved. Stir in chocolate pieces.
3. MICROWAVE (high), uncovered, 45–60 seconds or until chocolate is melted. Stir in vanilla and almond extract. Cool until mixture begins to thicken.
4. Prepare topping mix as directed on package. Fold chocolate mixture into whipped topping. Spoon into 6 sherbet glasses. Refrigerate until served. Garnish with sliced almonds, if desired.

PEACH MELBA

About 4 servings, 120 calories each

Fresh peaches combine with raspberry preserves for a pretty and delicious dessert. Serve with ice cream or plain.

2 **ripe peaches, halved and cored**

4 **teaspoons raspberry preserves**

4 **scoops vanilla ice cream**

1. Arrange peaches cut side down in four 5-ounce microwave-safe custard cups.
2. MICROWAVE (high), uncovered, 3½–4 minutes or until peaches are tender. Turn peaches cut side up. Spoon preserves into cavity of peaches. To serve, top with ice cream.

TIP

- Try a vanilla or almond-flavored tofu-type frozen dessert as a substitute for ice cream for lower calories and slightly higher nutritional value.

ANGEL CAKE WITH CHOCOLATE TOPPING

About 16 servings, 155 calories each

A lite milk chocolate topping makes the perfect finish for angel food cake.

¾ **cup skim milk**

¼ **cup sugar**

2 **tablespoons cornstarch**

1 **egg, beaten**

½ **square unsweetened chocolate**

½ **teaspoon vanilla**

3 **tablespoons margarine**

1 **12-inch round angel food cake**

1. Combine milk, sugar, and cornstarch in 1-quart microwave-safe mixing bowl. Mix well.
2. MICROWAVE (high), uncovered, 2–2½ minutes or until mixture boils and thickens, stirring once. Blend a small amount of mixture into beaten egg. Return to hot mixture. Add chocolate.
3. MICROWAVE (high), uncovered, 30–40 seconds or until bubbly around edge. Stir to melt chocolate. Blend in vanilla. Refrigerate until completely chilled, at least 6 hours.
4. Beat margarine until light and creamy. Gradually beat in chocolate mixture, continuing to beat until creamy, cut cake into 16 wedges and frost the uncut cake with chocolate mixture, or spoon a tablespoon of topping onto each slice.

TIP

● Diet margarine can be used; calories will be slightly lower.

SLICED CINNAMON APPLES

About 4 servings, 50 calories each

Red hot candies add flavor and a rosy color to these apple slices.

2 **large apples, cored and sliced**

4 **teaspoons red hot cinnamon candies**

1. Arrange apple slices in four 6-ounce microwave-safe custard cups. Sprinkle cinnamon candies on top.
2. MICROWAVE (high), uncovered, 7–8 minutes or until apples are tender and candies are melted, stirring once. Serve warm or cold.

TIP

● Apples can be peeled, if desired.

TOASTED COCONUT PUDDING

About 4 servings, 145 calories each

Toasted coconut is added to this creamy vanilla pudding.

¼ **cup flaked coconut**

1 **teaspoon water**

¼ **cup sugar**

1½ **tablespoons cornstarch**

1½ **cups skim milk**

1 **egg, beaten**

1 **teaspoon vanilla**

1. Combine coconut and water in 1-cup microwave-safe measure.
2. MICROWAVE (high), uncovered 2½–3 minutes or until lightly toasted, stirring several times. Set aside.
3. Combine sugar and cornstarch in 1-quart microwave-safe mixing bowl. Stir in milk and egg until well blended.
4. MICROWAVE (high), uncovered, 4–5 minutes or until mixture boils and thickens, stirring 2 or 3 times. Reserve 1 tablespoon coconut for garnish. Add remainder to pudding. Blend in vanilla. Pour into 4 serving dishes. Sprinkle with reserved coconut. Serve warm or cold.

TIP

• Almond extract can be substituted for vanilla.

VERY BERRY MOUSSE

About 8 servings, 100 calories each

A lite, melt-in-your-mouth dessert that is as pretty as it is good.

2 **cups fresh or thawed frozen raspberries or strawberries**

¼ **cup sugar**

2 **tablespoons cornstarch**

1 **envelope unflavored gelatin**

¾ **cup water**

1 **cup (8 ounces) vanilla yogurt**

1 **envelope whipped topping mix, prepared**

Fresh berries for garnish (optional)

1. Combine berries, sugar, cornstarch, and gelatin in 1-quart microwave-safe mixing bowl. Mix lightly. Stir in water.
2. MICROWAVE (high), uncovered, 5–6 minutes or until mixture boils and thickens, stirring twice. Cool.
3. Stir in yogurt. Prepare topping mix as directed on package. Fold into berry mixture. Spoon into 8 individual dishes or into one large serving dish. Refrigerate at least 5 hours. If desired, garnish with fresh berries.

CREAMY STRAWBERRY SOUFFLE

**About 4 servings,
140 calories each**

This dessert can also be served as a salad by omitting the garnish and serving the gelatin on a lettuce leaf. If desired, place a pineapple slice on the lettuce before adding the soufflé.

¾ *cup water*

1 *3-ounce package strawberry-flavored gelatin*

1 *cup fresh or frozen strawberries*

¾ *cup plain yogurt*

4 *strawberries*

1. MICROWAVE (high) water in uncovered 2-cup microwave-safe measure until boiling.

2. Stir in gelatin until dissolved. Cool 10 minutes. Pour mixture into blender or food processor container; add strawberries. Cover and process until smooth. Add ½ cup of yogurt (reserve remainder for topping); blend on low speed. Pour mixture into 4 custard cups or individual molds; chill several hours.

3. To serve, unmold onto dessert plates and garnish each serving with 1 tablespoon yogurt and a sliced strawberry.

QUICK FRUIT COBBLER

**About 6 servings,
125 calories each**

Here is a super-easy cobbler that uses fresh or frozen fruit.

4 *cups fresh fruit (apples, blueberries, peaches, boysenberries, or a combination), sliced as necessary*

¼ *cup sugar*

¼ *cup flour*

2 *tablespoons margarine*

Ground cinnamon

1. Place fruit in shallow 1-quart microwave-safe baking dish. Sprinkle evenly with a mixture of sugar and flour. Cut margarine into thin slices. Arrange slices over flour mixture. Sprinkle with cinnamon.

2. MICROWAVE (high), uncovered, 7–9 minutes or until fruit is tender, rotating dish once. Serve warm.

TIP

● When using frozen fruit, increase time to 11–12 minutes.

FRUIT KABOBS

**About 5 servings,
55 calories each**

These colorful kabobs are coated with an easy orange glaze to enhance the flavor.

**2 tablespoons orange
marmalade**

1 apple, peeled if desired

1 medium banana

1 orange

2 tablespoons flaked coconut

5 10-inch wooden skewers

1. MICROWAVE (high) marmalade in uncovered 2-cup microwave-safe measure 45–60 seconds or until hot, stirring once. Quarter and core apple; cut into chunks. Peel banana and cut into chunks. Add apple and banana to marmalade; mix lightly to coat evenly. Peel and section orange; cut sections in half. Add to apple and banana. Divide fruit among 5 skewers. Brush with remaining marmalade. Sprinkle with coconut. Place kabobs on microwave-safe plate.

2. MICROWAVE (high), uncovered, 1½–2 minutes or until heated through.

TIP

● Kabobs can be served cold.

LEMONY PEAR DELIGHT

**About 4 servings,
115 calories each**

Pears and lemon pudding team to make a tangy, refreshing dessert.

¼ cup sugar

3 tablespoons cornstarch

1 cup water

1 egg, slightly beaten

¼ cup lemon juice

**¼ teaspoon butter flavoring
(optional)**

¼ cup granola cereal

**1 16-ounce can pear halves in
fruit juice, drained**

1. Combine sugar and cornstarch in 2-cup microwave-safe measure. Stir in water.

2. MICROWAVE (high), uncovered, 2½–3½ minutes or until mixture boils and thickens, stirring once. Blend a small amount of hot mixture into egg. Return to hot mixture, blending well.

3. MICROWAVE (high), uncovered, 30–45 seconds or until bubbly around edge, stirring once. Stir in lemon juice and butter flavoring. Cool slightly.

4. Sprinkle ½ tablespoon granola into each of 4 sherbet dishes. Top each with pear half, cut side down. Pour lemon pudding over pears. Sprinkle with remaining granola.

TIP

● Granola can be omitted. Top with sliced fresh strawberries, kiwifruit, or blueberries.

CREAMY STRAWBERRY TAPIOCA

**About 8 servings,
90 calories each**

This lite and creamy fruit tapioca is sure to be an often requested dessert.

1½ **cups water**

¼ **cup quick-cooking tapioca**

¼ **cup sugar**

2 **cups whole strawberries,
chopped**

1 **envelope whipped topping
mix, prepared**

1. Combine water, tapioca, and sugar in 1-quart microwave-safe mixing bowl.
2. MICROWAVE (high), uncovered, 4½–5½ minutes or until mixture boils, stirring once. Cool. Add strawberries. Prepare whipped topping mix as directed on package. Fold into cooled pudding. Refrigerate until served.

TIPS

- Frozen strawberries can be used. Thaw just enough to chop, then add them to the warm pudding to speed cooling.

- Other favorite berries can be substituted. Raspberries, blueberries, or boysenberries are delicious.

- Thawed, frozen whipped topping can be substituted for topping mix; use 2 cups. Calories will be slightly higher.

BANANA SPLITS

**About 2 servings,
130 calories each**

Banana halves are topped with a light chocolate syrup, whipped topping, and pecans. A scoop of ice milk makes this even better!

½ **ounce semisweet chocolate
(half a square)**

½ **tablespoon light corn syrup**

½ **tablespoon skim milk**

¼ **teaspoon vanilla**

1 **small banana, split lengthwise**

2 **tablespoons thawed frozen
whipped topping**

1 **tablespoon chopped pecans**

1. Combine chocolate, corn syrup, and milk in 1-cup microwave-safe measure.
2. MICROWAVE (high), uncovered, 45–60 seconds or until chocolate is melted, stirring once. Stir in vanilla; set aside.
3. Place a banana half in each of 2 serving dishes. Top with chocolate sauce, whipped topping, and pecans.

TIP

- A scoop of favorite ice milk or tofu-type frozen dessert can be added before whipped topping. Calories will be higher.

CHOCOLITE DESSERT

**2 servings,
125 calories each**

Enjoy this lite and creamy version of pots de crème. See the "Tips" for increasing the quantity.

⅓ **cup skim milk**

¼ **teaspoon unflavored gelatin**

¼ **cup milk chocolate pieces**

¼ **teaspoon vanilla**

1 egg white

Dash cream of tartar

1. Combine milk and gelatin in 2-cup microwave-safe measure. Let stand 2–3 minutes to soften gelatin.

2. MICROWAVE (high), uncovered, 1–1½ minutes or until steaming hot. Stir in chocolate pieces and vanilla until chocolate is melted. Refrigerate until mixture begins to thicken, 30–45 minutes.

3. Beat egg white and cream of tartar until mixture forms soft peaks. Gently fold in chocolate mixture. Spoon into 2 dessert dishes. Refrigerate until set, at least 1 hour.

TIPS

- Recipe can be doubled or tripled. When doubled, increase time in step 2 to 2–2½ minutes. When tripled, increase time to 3–4 minutes.

- If egg white is warmed slightly, it will whip to greater volume. You can do this in the microwave by microwaving it 5–8 seconds before beating. Be sure that you do not start cooking it.

BERRY-FILLED ANGEL FOOD

**About 12 servings,
145 calories each**

Frozen strawberries and a ready-made angel food cake are teamed in this delicious, lite dessert. The recipe makes 12 servings, but extras can be refrigerated or frozen for another meal.

1 10-ounce package frozen quick-thaw lite strawberries

2 tablespoons water

1 teaspoon unflavored gelatin

1 loaf angel food cake (about 9 ounces)

½ cup thawed frozen whipped topping

1. MICROWAVE (high) strawberries in package 1–1½ minutes or until almost thawed, rearranging berries once. Set aside. Combine water and gelatin in 2-cup microwave-safe measure. Let stand a few minutes to soften.

2. MICROWAVE (high), uncovered, 30–45 seconds or until boiling. Stir to dissolve gelatin. Add strawberries; mix well. Place in freezer for 5–10 minutes or until partially set.

3. Cut cake in half horizontally. Remove top layer. Spread 1 cup of strawberry mixture on cut side of one layer. Top with remaining layer. Fold whipped topping into remaining strawberry mixture. Spoon onto top of cake. Refrigerate until served.

TIPS

- Frozen sweetened sliced strawberries can be substituted for the lite berries. Calories will be slightly higher. Or use about 2 cups frozen unsweetened strawberries and add about 2 tablespoons sugar.

- Pound cake can be substituted for angel food cake. Calories will be higher.

CHERRY-ALMOND-TOPPED FROZEN YOGURT

About 4 servings, 150 calories each

Try this yummy topping over vanilla, peach, or chocolate frozen yogurt; you'll like them all.

1 cup lite prepared cherry pie filling

¼ teaspoon almond extract

⅛ teaspoon ground cinnamon

1 pint frozen yogurt

1. MICROWAVE (high) pie filling in uncovered 2-cup microwave-safe measure 1½–2 minutes or until hot. Stir in extract and cinnamon.

2. Spoon about ½ cup frozen yogurt into each of 4 serving dishes. Top each with about ¼ cup warm cherry mixture.

TIPS

● Other flavors of pie filling can be substituted.

● There are about 2 cups pie filling in a can; the extra can be frozen for use another time, or you can make a double recipe and keep it in the refrigerator. Just warm 2–3 minutes before serving.

PEACHES FLAMBE

About 4 servings, 130 calories each

A delicious and pretty dessert. Try it over cake, too.

1½ cups frozen unsweetened sliced peaches

1 tablespoon brown sugar

½ teaspoon lemon juice

1 pint vanilla ice milk

1 tablespoon brandy

1. Combine peaches and brown sugar in 20-ounce microwave-safe casserole. Cover with casserole lid.

2. MICROWAVE (high) 3½–4 minutes or until tender, stirring once. Stir in lemon juice.

3. Spoon about ½ cup ice milk into each of 4 serving dishes. Spoon warm peach mixture over ice milk.

4. To flame dessert, MICROWAVE (high) brandy in 1-cup glass measure 10–15 seconds. Carefully ignite with match and pour over peach mixture just before serving. Spoon warm peach mixture over ice milk.

TIPS

● To save time when serving, spoon ice milk into dishes ahead of time and place in freezer.

● When not flaming dessert, brandy can be omitted and ½ teaspoon brandy extract added with lemon juice in step 2.

APPLE BARS

**About 20 bars,
80 calories each**

These moist and spicy apple bars are a welcome addition to many meals. They also make tasty snacks or lunch box treats.

2 medium apples, cored and
  chopped (about 2 cups)

1 egg

½ cup packed brown sugar

¼ cup cooking oil

¾ cup unsifted whole wheat
  flour

1 teaspoon ground cinnamon

½ teaspoon soda

¼ teaspoon salt

Powdered sugar (optional)

1. Combine all ingredients except powdered sugar in food processor container. Process at medium speed until thoroughly combined.

2. Grease bottom only of 10- by 6-inch microwave-safe baking dish. Spread batter evenly in dish. Cover with plastic wrap.

3. MICROWAVE (high) 5½–6½ minutes or until no longer doughy, rotating dish once. Cool; if desired, sprinkle with powdered sugar.

TIP

● If food processor is not available, finely chop apple and mix with other ingredients until combined.

FRUIT CREAM

**About 6 servings,
135 calories each**

Early summer fruit is delicious in this smooth and creamy dessert. Vary the flavor of gelatin and use other fruits in season throughout the summer.

1 cup water

1 3-ounce package strawberry-
  flavored gelatin

2 cups ice milk

1 cup sliced fresh strawberries

1. MICROWAVE (high) water in uncovered 1-quart microwave-safe mixing bowl 2½–3½ minutes or until it boils.

2. Stir in gelatin until dissolved. Spoon ice milk into gelatin; stir until melted. Pour over fruit in individual serving dishes or in a serving bowl. Cover and refrigerate until set, at least 4 hours.

TIP

● Sugar-free gelatin can be substituted for regular gelatin. Calories will be lower.

ORANGE CHIFFON PIE

**About 10 servings,
165 calories each**

*This lite but luscious citrus pie is sure to be a favorite. Even desserts like pie can be a
part of lite dining when the filling is airy and the servings are somewhat slim.*

1 unbaked pastry shell

¼ cup sugar

1 envelope unflavored gelatin

4 eggs, separated

⅔ cup water

¼ cup orange juice

1 tablespoon grated orange peel

½ teaspoon cream of tartar

¼ cup sugar

1. MICROWAVE (high) pastry shell in uncovered 9-inch microwave-safe pie plate 6–7 minutes or until no longer doughy, rotating plate once or twice. Set aside to cool.

2. Stir together ¼ cup sugar and the gelatin in 1-quart microwave-safe mixing bowl. Blend in egg yolks, water, and orange juice, mixing well.

3. MICROWAVE (high), uncovered, 3½–4 minutes or until mixture boils, stirring 2 or 3 times. Stir in orange peel. Place bowl in another bowl of ice water or refrigerate until mixture mounds slightly, stirring occasionally.

4. Beat egg whites and cream of tartar until frothy. Gradually beat in ¼ cup sugar until stiff peaks form. Fold into orange mixture. Pile into baked pastry shell. Refrigerate 2–3 hours or until set.

TIPS

- Substitute lime juice and a little green food coloring to make Lime Chiffon Pie.

- If desired, eliminate the crust and serve chiffon in a pretty serving dish. For 10 servings, calories will be about 75 each.

BERRY CREME SQUARES

**About 10 servings,
110 calories each**

This delicious strawberry dessert is like a trifle, but served in squares.

½ **unfrosted yellow cake layer, cubed (about 4 cups)**

3 **tablespoons sugar**

1 **tablespoon cornstarch**

1 **teaspoon unflavored gelatin**

1 **cup skim milk**

1 **egg, beaten**

½ **teaspoon almond extract**

2 **cups (1 pint) sliced fresh strawberries**

1 **envelope whipped topping mix, prepared**

10 **whole strawberries or mint sprigs for garnish (optional)**

1. Layer cake cubes in 10- by 6-inch baking dish. Set aside. Combine sugar, cornstarch, gelatin, and skim milk in 4-cup microwave-safe measure. Mix well.

2. MICROWAVE (high), uncovered, 3½–4 minutes or until mixture boils and thickens slightly, stirring once. Blend a small amount of mixture into beaten egg; return to hot mixture, blending well.

3. MICROWAVE (high), uncovered, 30–60 seconds or until bubbly around edges, stirring once. Stir in almond extract. Pour over cake cubes. Cool 15 minutes.

4. Layer strawberries over cooled pudding. Prepare whipped topping as directed on package, substituting almond extract for vanilla. Spread over strawberries. Cover and refrigerate up to 24 hours.

5. *To Serve:* Cut into serving pieces. If desired, garnish each with a whole strawberry or a mint sprig.

LITE AND LOVELY CHEESECAKE

**About 10 servings,
150 calories each**

Serve this cheesecake often, topped with favorite in-season fruits. It is very light and creamy.

1 12-ounce carton low-fat
cottage cheese (1½ cups)

4 ounces Neufchâtel cheese

½ cup sugar

3 eggs

1 envelope unflavored gelatin

⅔ cup skim milk

1 teaspoon vanilla

½ tablespoon margarine

½ cup graham cracker crumbs

Fresh fruit for garnish
(optional)

1. Process cottage cheese in blender or food processor container until smooth. Blend in Neufchâtel cheese, sugar, eggs, and gelatin; process until smooth. Blend in milk. Transfer to 1-quart microwave-safe mixing bowl.

2. MICROWAVE (high), uncovered, 5½–6½ minutes or until steaming hot and slightly thickened, stirring 2 or 3 times. Stir in vanilla. Set aside to cool slightly.

3. MICROWAVE (high) margarine in uncovered 8-inch round microwave-safe baking dish 30–60 seconds or until melted. Mix in cracker crumbs; press evenly into bottom of baking dish. Pour slightly cooled cheesecake mixture into dish. Refrigerate until set, about 4 hours. Garnish with fresh fruit if desired.

PIÑA COLADA SHERBET

**About 6 servings,
60 calories each**

Pineapple and coconut flavoring combine in this refreshing summer dessert.

1 20-ounce can crushed
pineapple in fruit juice

¼ cup sugar

1 teaspoon unflavored gelatin

½ teaspoon coconut extract

1. Drain pineapple, reserving juice. Combine juice and sugar in 2-cup microwave-safe measure. Sprinkle with gelatin. Let stand 2–3 minutes.

2. MICROWAVE (high), uncovered, 2–2½ minutes or until mixture boils vigorously and sugar and gelatin are dissolved, stirring once. Combine with pineapple and remaining ingredients. Pour into 13- by 9-inch baking pan. Freeze until frozen around edges. Transfer to mixer bowl. Beat at medium speed until smooth and creamy. Spoon into freezer container. Cover tightly, label, and freeze up to 1 month.

3. *To Serve:* Remove from freezer and let stand 15–20 minutes. Spoon into sherbet glasses.

TIP

• If coconut extract is not available, substitute almond extract. Add 2 tablespoons flaked coconut with pineapple. Calories will be higher.

BLUEBERRY-CHEESE CRUNCH

**About 6 servings,
125 calories each**

Lightly sweetened blueberries are topped with a cheese mixture and crunchy cubes.

*2 cups frozen unsweetened
blueberries (about 12 ounces)*

¼ cup sugar

1 tablespoon cornstarch

½ cup water

1 tablespoon Grand Marnier

1 tablespoon margarine

2 teaspoons sugar

Dash ground cinnamon

1 slice bread, cubed

2 ounces Neufchâtel cheese

1. Combine blueberries and ¼ cup sugar in 1-quart microwave-safe mixing bowl.

2. MICROWAVE (high), uncovered, 2½–3 minutes or until thawed, stirring once. Combine cornstarch and water in 2-cup microwave-safe measure. Drain juices from berries into cup; mix well.

3. MICROWAVE (high), uncovered, 3–4 minutes or until mixture boils and thickens, stirring once or twice. Pour over berries. Stir in Grand Marnier.

4. MICROWAVE (high) margarine in 2-cup microwave-safe measure 30–45 seconds or until melted. Stir in 2 teaspoons sugar, cinnamon, and bread pieces until evenly coated.

5. MICROWAVE (high), uncovered, 1½–2 mintues or until bread is crisp, stirring once. Cool.

6. MICROWAVE (high) cheese in small uncovered microwave-safe dish 30–45 seconds or until softened; set aside. Spoon berries into 6 serving dishes; top each with about 1 teaspoon cheese. Cover and refrigerate until served. Just before serving, sprinkle with bread cubes.

TIP

● Fresh blueberries can be substituted. Reduce cooking time in step 2 to 1–1½ minutes or until juicy.

CREAM-IN-THE-MIDDLE CAKE

About 12 servings, 150 calories each

Chocolate cake, raspberry preserves, and butter-cream filling are combined in this yummy dessert.

½ **18.5-ounce package chocolate cake mix (2-layer size), prepared**

¼ **cup skim milk**

1 **tablespoon flour**

¼ **cup margarine**

2 **tablespoons sugar**

¼ **teaspoon vanilla**

2 **tablespoons raspberry or strawberry preserves**

Powdered sugar

1. Prepare cake mix as directed on package using half the ingredient amounts. Grease bottom only of 8-inch round microwave-safe baking dish. Pour batter into dish; spread evenly.

2. MICROWAVE (medium—50%), uncovered, 5–6 minutes or until edges are set, rotating dish once. Then MICROWAVE (high) 1–2 minutes or until no longer doughy. Cool 10 minutes; invert onto cooling rack and cool completely.

3. Combine milk and flour in 1-cup microwave-safe measure; stir until smooth.

4. MICROWAVE (high), uncovered, 45–60 seconds or until mixture boils and thickens, stirring once. Refrigerate 15–20 minutes or until chilled.

5. MICROWAVE (high) margarine in uncovered small microwave-safe mixer bowl 15–20 seconds or just until soft. Beat in sugar and vanilla until creamy. Gradually beat in flour mixture, beating until fluffy.

6. Slice cake layer in half horizontally using serrated knife. Place bottom piece on serving plate cut side up. Spread with preserves and then filling. Top with remaining cake layer, cut side down. Sprinkle with powdered sugar. Cover and refrigerate up to 24 hours.

TIPS

- One-layer cake mixes can be used, but the 2-layer mixes usually microwave with better results. Two layers can be cooked and the second frozen for later use.

- If cake layer is refrigerated, it will be easier to cut and fill.

- Other favorite flavors of cake mix can be substituted.

- To use full power instead of the lower power setting in step 2, MICROWAVE 5–6 minutes, rotating dish twice, and omit second microwaving in step 2.

COOL LIME SOUFFLE

**About 8 servings,
130 calories each**

"Lite yet fancy" describes this chilled dessert that adds an elegant touch to any meal.

1 envelope unflavored gelatin

¼ cup sugar

1 cup skim milk

3 eggs, separated

1 tablespoon grated lime peel

⅓ cup fresh lime juice

3–4 drops green food coloring

¼ teaspoon cream of tartar

¼ cup sugar

1 envelope whipped topping
  mix, prepared

Lime slices for garnish
(optional)

1. Cut a 3-inch collar of waxed paper to fit inside 4-cup soufflé dish. Lightly grease top inside edge of dish; fit paper against dish, allowing paper to extend about 2 inches above dish. Set aside.

2. Combine gelatin, ¼ cup sugar, milk, and egg yolks in 2-cup microwave-safe measure. Beat until smooth.

3. MICROWAVE (high), uncovered, 2–3 minutes or until mixture just begins to bubble, stirring twice during last half of cooking time. Beat until smooth. Stir in lime peel, juice, and coloring. Refrigerate until slightly thickened, about 1 hour.

4. Beat egg whites and cream of tartar until frothy. Gradually beat in ¼ cup sugar until stiff peaks form. Prepare whipped topping mix as directed on package. Fold whipped topping and gelatin into egg whites. Spoon into prepared dish. Refrigerate at least 4 hours or until served.

5. *To Serve:* Carefully remove collar. If desired, garnish top with lime slices.

BANANA-ORANGE PUSH-UPS

**8 push-ups,
125 calories each**

Have this refreshing combination of banana and orange ready in the freezer. It's a quick pick-me-up snack especially suited to warm summer days.

1 6-ounce can frozen orange
  juice concentrate

2 ripe bananas

1 cup plain yogurt

½ cup instant nonfat dry milk
  granules

½ cup water

¼ cup sugar

8 paper cups

8 wooden Popsicle sticks

1. Combine all ingredients (except cups and sticks) in blender or food processor container. Blend until frothy. Pour into 8 paper cups. Cover with foil. Make slit in center of foil; insert Popsicle stick into each. Freeze up to 3 months.

2. *To Serve:* Remove foil and peel off paper cup.

PEPPERMINT FLUFF PIE

**About 8 servings,
90 calories each**

Peppermint adds a refreshing finish to a hearty meal. When you taste it, you will never believe it has so few calories.

2 tablespoons margarine

1 cup crushed chocolate wafers (about 15)

1 tablespoon sugar

1½ teaspoons unflavored gelatin

¼ cup water

¾ cup skim milk

3 tablespoons sugar

⅛ teaspoon peppermint extract

4 egg whites

3 tablespoons sugar

3–4 drops red food coloring

2 tablespoons crushed peppermint candy

1. MICROWAVE (high) margarine in 9-inch microwave-safe pie plate 30–45 seconds or until melted. Stir in wafers and 1 tablespoon sugar. Press into bottom and up sides of plate.

2. MICROWAVE (high), uncovered, 1½–2 minutes or until heated, rotating plate once.

3. Add gelatin to water. Let stand a few minutes to soften.

4. MICROWAVE (high) milk in uncovered 2-cup microwave-safe measure 2–2½ minutes or until steaming hot. Stir in softened gelatin, 3 tablespoons sugar, and extract until dissolved. Refrigerate until mixture starts to thicken, about 1 hour.

5. Beat egg whites until frothy. Gradually beat in 3 tablespoons sugar until mixture forms stiff peaks. Beat gelatin mixture until smooth. Fold gelatin mixture into beaten egg whites. Fold in food coloring. Spoon into crumb crust. Cover and refrigerate until set, at least 3 hours. Just before serving, sprinkle with crushed candy.

TIPS

• Crushed candy can be omitted. If desired, sprinkle top of pie with a little of the mixture for the crumb crust.

• To cover the pie without having the covering stick to the pie filling, first insert 4 or 5 toothpicks into pie filling. Then place covering on so it rests on the toothpicks rather than the filling.

LEMONY LITE PIE

**About 12 servings,
125 calories each**

You'll find this lite and airy frozen pie pleasantly tart and delightfully refreshing.

3 tablespoons margarine

1 cup graham cracker crumbs

2 eggs, separated

¼ cup sugar

1 teaspoon grated lemon peel

¼ cup lemon juice

¼ cup sugar

1 envelope whipped topping
   mix, prepared

1. MICROWAVE (high) margarine in uncovered 9-inch microwave-safe pie plate 30–60 seconds or until melted. Stir in crumbs. Press into bottom and up sides of dish.

2. MICROWAVE (high), uncovered, 1½–2 minutes or until heated, rotating plate once. Set aside. Combine egg yolks, ¼ cup sugar, lemon peel, and juice in 1-quart microwave-safe mixing bowl; beat until light.

3. MICROWAVE (high), uncovered, 1½–2½ minutes or until slightly thickened, stirring twice. Refrigerate until cool, about 30 minutes.

4. Beat egg whites until frothy. Gradually add ¼ cup sugar, beating until mixture forms soft peaks. Set aside.

5. Prepare whipped topping mix as directed on package. Fold topping and egg whites into cooled lemon mixture. Carefully pour into crust. Cover, label, and freeze until firm or up to 1 month. Remove from freezer about 15 minutes before serving time.

TIPS

- Orange peel and juice can be substituted to make an orange pie, or use lime peel and juice for a lime pie.

- Thawed frozen whipped topping can be substituted for topping mix; use 2 cups. Calories will be slightly higher.

- To speed cooling process, place the lemon mixture in the freezer for about 10 minutes or set dish in another dish of ice water.

FROZEN STRAWBERRY CREAM

**About 9 servings,
125 calories each**

This dessert is so good that it is hard to believe it has so few calories!

2 tablespoons margarine

1 tablespoon sugar

¾ cup graham cracker crumbs

1 teaspoon unflavored gelatin

2 tablespoons cold water

2 egg whites

¼ cup sugar

2 tablespoons lemon juice

2 cups crushed fresh
strawberries (about 1½ pints)

1 envelope whipped topping
mix, prepared

1. MICROWAVE (high) margarine in uncovered 8-by 8-inch microwave-safe baking dish 30–45 seconds or until melted. Stir in 1 tablespoon sugar and the crumbs. Press into bottom of dish.

2. Sprinkle gelatin over water. Let stand a couple of minutes to soften.

3. MICROWAVE (high), uncovered, 30–45 seconds or until gelatin is dissolved. Set aside to cool.

4. Combine egg whites, ¼ cup sugar, lemon juice, and strawberries in large mixer bowl. Beat at medium speed about 10 minutes or until mixture is very thick. Beat in gelatin. Prepare whipped topping as directed on package. Fold into strawberry mixture. Pour into crust. Cover, label, and freeze until firm or up to 1 month. Remove from freezer about 15 minutes before serving.

TIPS

● Frozen strawberries can be used; just MICROWAVE (high) 30–45 seconds or until partially thawed.

● Other berries such as raspberries, boysenberries, or blueberries can be substituted for strawberries.

DOUBLE CHOCOLATE-ALMOND DELIGHT

About 12 servings, 130 calories each

Here's a delightful frozen dessert that has a rich chocolate flavor but is low in calories.

   2 *tablespoons margarine*

  28 *chocolate wafers, crushed fine (2 cups)*

   1 *envelope whipped topping mix*

   1 *pint Dutch chocolate almond tofu-type frozen dessert*

1. MICROWAVE (high) margarine in uncovered 10-by 6-inch microwave-safe baking dish 30–45 seconds or until melted. Mix in wafers until evenly coated. Reserve 1 tablespoon for topping. Press remainder into bottom of dish.

2. MICROWAVE (high), uncovered, 1½–2 minutes or until heated through, rotating dish once. Set aside. Prepare whipped topping mix as directed on package.

3. MICROWAVE (high) tofu dessert 1½–2 minutes or until softened; fold into whipped topping. Spoon onto crust; spread evenly. Sprinkle with reserved crumbs. Cover tightly and freeze up to 1 month.

4. *To Serve:* Remove from freezer about 10 minutes before serving. Cut into serving pieces.

TIP

• Other flavors of tofu-type frozen dessert can be substituted. Select a flavor that will be enhanced by the chocolate crust.

FROZEN YOGURT CUPS

**6 cups,
70 calories each**

Fruit cocktail teams with yogurt for a refreshing lite dessert.

1 8-ounce can fruit cocktail

1 teaspoon cornstarch

*1 cup strawberry-flavored
yogurt*

3 maraschino cherries, halved

1. Drain juice from fruit cocktail into 2-cup microwave-safe measure. Blend in cornstarch.
2. MICROWAVE (high), uncovered, 1½–1¾ minutes or until mixture boils and thickens, stirring once. Cool.
3. Blend yogurt into cooled sauce; stir in fruit cocktail. Line 6 muffin cups with paper liners. Spoon mixture into cups. Top each with ½ cherry. Freeze until firm. Place in freezer bag or container. Cover, label, and freeze up to 2 months.
4. *To Serve:* Allow cups to stand at room temperature about 15 minutes. Remove papers and place cups on individual serving plates.

TIPS

- Two tablespoons chopped nuts can be added to mixture with yogurt. Calories will be slightly higher.

- Canned sliced peaches or pears can be substituted for fruit cocktail.

ORANGE SORBET

**4 servings,
95 calories each**

The orange shells make attractive holders for this refreshing fresh fruit sorbet.

2 oranges, halved

¾ cup water

⅓ cup sugar

1 teaspoon unflavored gelatin

1 tablespoon lemon juice

1. Squeeze juice from oranges into 1-quart microwave-safe mixing bowl. Set aside empty shells. Add water and sugar to orange juice.
2. MICROWAVE (high), uncovered, 2½–3½ minutes or until mixture boils. Stir and then MICROWAVE (high) 1 minute longer. Dissolve gelatin in lemon juice. Let stand 2 minutes. Stir into hot orange juice, stirring until dissolved. Pour into 13- by 9-inch baking pan. Freeze until crystals set around edge, about 3 hours.
3. Transfer frozen mixture to chilled mixer bowl. Beat at medium speed until fluffy. Spoon into orange shells, piling high. Return to freezer. Once firmly frozen, wrap, label, and freeze.
4. *To Serve:* Unwrap desired number of servings and allow to stand at room temperature 10–15 minutes before serving.

INDEX

All-American Pizza, 44
Ambrosia Cups, 93
Ambrosia Oranges, 69
Angel Cake with Chocolate
    Topping, 209
Angel Food, Berry-Filled, 215
Apple
    Apple Bars, 217
    Apple-Bran Coffeecake, 17
    Apple-Bran Muffins, 143
    Apple S'mores, 73
    Apples and Cheese, 131
    Sliced Cinnamon Apples, 209
Asparagus
    Asparagus and Beef Vinaigrette,
        82
    Asparagus and Carrots, 93
    Asparagus Omelet, 80
    Carrot-Asparagus Duo, 51
Aspic Salads, Tomato, 151

Bacon, Canadian, 19
Bacon Cheeseburgers, 100
Bacon-Tomato Sandwiches, 148
Bacon-Topped Tomato Slices, 135
Banana-Date Oatmeal, 11
Banana-Orange Push-Ups, 223
Banana Splits, 213
Bars
    Apple Bars, 217
    Carrot Bars, 89
    Granola Bars, 76
Beef. See also Ground Beef
    Asparagus and Beef Vinaigrette,
        82
    Pepper Steak, 188
    Skewered Beef Teriyaki, 168

Sliced Beef with Mustard Sauce,
    166
Steak Diane, 118
Stroganoff for Two, 102
Swiss Steak, 190
Beefy Meatball Minestrone, 42
Berry Cream Squares, 219
Berry-Filled Angel Food, 215
Beverages
    Cinnamon Coffee, 15
    Cranberry Fizz, 181
    Lo-Cal Strawberry Milk Shake,
        77
    Mocha Coffee, 27
    Orange Whip, 11
    Spiced Orange Tea, 21
    Zippy Tomato Drink, 13
Blueberry-Cheese Crunch, 221
Blueberry Shortstacks, 26
Bran Muffins, Top-of-the Morning,
    25
Breads. See also Muffins,
    Coffeecake
    Cheesy Wedges, 41
    Garlic Sticks, 33
    Parmesan Italian Bread, 157
    Pita Triangles, 161
    Poppy Seed Bread, 59
    Quick Garlic Rolls, 95
    Toasted Garlic Sticks, 145
Broccoli
    Broccoli Amandine, 137
    Broccoli-Ham Quiche, 162
    Calico Ham Slices, 142
    Cheesy Broccoli Chicken, 196
    Easy Broccoli, 199
    Fresh Vegetable Platter, 155

Marinated Vegetable Medley, 173
    Sesame Broccoli and Carrots, 37
Buttered New Potatoes, 61

Cabbage
    Cabbage Medley, 131
    Freezer Coleslaw, 183
    Hot Slaw, 125
Caesar Salad, Lite, 49
Cakes
    Angel Cake with Chocolate
        Topping, 209
    Berry Cream Squares, 219
    Berry-Filled Angel Food, 215
    Cream-in-the-Middle Cake, 222
Calico Ham Slices, 142
Canadian Bacon, 19
Caramel Flan, 207
Carrots
    Asparagus and Carrots, 93
    Carrot-Asparagus Duo, 51
    Carrot Bars, 89
    Carrot Coins, 39
    Pea Pods and Carrots, 169
    Sesame Broccoli and Carrots, 37
    Sherried Carrots, 171
    Tarragon Carrots and Zucchini,
        103
Cauliflower
    Fresh Vegetable Platter, 155
    Marinated Vegetable Medley, 173
Cheeseburgers, Bacon, 100
Cheesecake
    Individual Cheesecakes, 67
    Light and Lovely Cheesecake, 220
Cheesy Broccoli Chicken, 196
Cheesy Eggs with Bacon, 22

Cheesy Peach Halves, 43
Cheesy Vegetables, 129
Cheesy Wedges, 41
Cherry-Almond-Topped Frozen Yogurt, 216
Chicken
  Chicken à L'Orange, 46
  Chicken à la King, 198
  Chicken and Rice Soup, 56
  Chicken and Veggie Bundles, 104
  Cheesy Broccoli Chicken, 196
  Chicken Kiev, 203
  Chicken Nuggets, 126
  Chicken Stir-Fry, 109
  Chicken-Stuffed Potatoes, 128
  Chicken-Vegetable Rice Mold, 156
  Chicken with Waldorf Stuffing, 48
  Ching Chang Salad, 68
  French Chicken Strips, 60
  Moo Goo Gai Pan, 52
  Paella, 160
  Peasant Chicken, 106
  Savory Chicken Rolls, 50
  Tarragon Chicken, 86
Chili, 64
Ching Chang Salad, 68
Chocolate
  Angel Cake with Chocolate Topping, 209
  Chocolate-Almond Soufflé, 208
  Chocolite Dessert, 214
  Double Chocolate-Almond Delight, 227
Chunky Potato Salad, 167
Cinnamon Coffee, 15
Clam Chowder, Vegetable-, 78
Cobbler, Quick Fruit, 211
Cod Bella Vista, 130
Coffee
  Cinnamon Coffee, 15
  Mocha Coffee, 27
Coffeecake, Apple-Bran, 17
Coleslaw, Freezer, 183
Colorful Macaroni and Cheese, 54
Colorful Stuffed Peppers, 164
Cookware, 5
Cool Lime Soufflé, 223
Cordon Bleu, Turkey, 154
Corn Bread Muffins, 43
Crabmeat Sandwiches, Hot, 147
Cranberry Fizz, 181
Cream-in-the-Middle Cake, 222
Creamy Almond Custard, 207

Creamy Potato Puffs, 189
Creamy Strawberry Soufflé, 211
Creamy Strawberry Tapioca, 213
Creamy Zucchini Soup, 146
Cucumber Sauce, Salmon Timbales with, 136

Day Starters, 9
Desserts. See also individual types, 205
  Frozen Fruit Delites, 81
  Individual Cheesecakes, 67
  Lite Dessert Sauce, 85
  Pear Crisp, 79
Dilled Fresh Peas, 113
Dilly New Potatoes, 31
Double Chocolate-Almond Delight, 227

Easy Broccoli, 199
Easy Strawberry Jam, 28
Egg Drop Soup, 108
Eggs
  Asparagus Omelet, 80
  Cheesy Eggs with Bacon, 22
  Eggs Mexicana, 92
  Ham and Egg Sandwich Cups, 14
  Mexican Egg Roll-Ups, 12
  Morning Frittata, 20
  Scrambled Muffinwiches, 180
  Vegetarian Omelet, 74

Fajitas, Lemony Shrimp, 34
Family Meals, 29
Fettucchini with Vegetables, 94
Fish. See also individual types
  Cod Bella Vista, 130
  Fish Fillet Roll-Ups, 36
  Fish with Creole Rice, 112
  Golden Fish Nuggets, 110
  Sole Oscar, 30
  Stuffed Dilled Sole, 114
Flan, Caramel, 207
Florentine Lasagna Roll-Ups, 58
Florentine Rolls, 152
Fluffy Parsleyed Rice, 53
Fluffy White Rice, 197
Freezer Coleslaw, 183
Freezer Meals, 175
Freezer Meatballs, 177
Freezer Twice-Baked Potatoes, 191
French Bread Pizzas, 184
French Chicken Strips, 60
French-Cut Green Beans, 187
Fresh Fruit Gelatin Salad, 55

Fresh Vegetable Platter, 155
Frittata, Morning, 20
Frozen Fruit Delites, 81
Frozen Mini Fruit Salads, 185
Frozen Strawberry Cream, 226
Frozen Yogurt Cups, 228
Fruit. See also individual types
  Ambrosia Cups, 93
  Ambrosia Oranges, 69
  Frozen Fruit Delites, 81
  Frozen Mini Fruit Salads, 185
  Frozen Yogurt Cups, 228
  Fruit Cream, 217
  Fruit Kabobs, 212
  Fruit-Nut Balls, 71
  Glazed Fresh Fruit, 87
  Glased Fruit Bowl, 23
  Lemon-Sauced Kiwifruit and Strawberries, 206
  Lite Yogurt Salad, 123
  Oriental Fruit Compote, 141
  Quick Fruit Cobbler, 211
  Sugar-Glazed Grapefruit, 24
  Summertime Fruit Cup, 75
  Yogurt-Fruit Bowl, 16
Fruit Cream, 217

Garlic Sticks, 33
Glazed Fresh Fruit, 87
Glazed Fruit Bowl, 23
Golden Fish Nuggets, 110
Granola Bars, 76
Granola, Yogurt and, 83
Grapefruit, Sugar-Glazed, 24
Green Beans
  French-Cut Green Beans, 187
  Green Bean-Filled Tomatoes, 120
  Green Bean Moussaka, 40
  Lemon-Lite Green Beans, 101
  Quick Creamy Beans, 97
  Savory Italian Green Beans, 133
Ground Beef
  Bacon Cheeseburgers, 100
  Beefy Meatball Minestrone, 42
  Chili, 64
  Colorful Stuffed Peppers, 164
  Florentine Rolls, 152
  Freezer Meatballs, 177
  French Bread Pizzas, 184
  Green Bean Moussaka, 40
  Individual Meat Loaves, 98
  Meatball Stroganoff, 177
  Meatballs Bourguignon, 179
  Meatballs with Spaghetti Sauce, 178

Mexican Spoon Tacos, 186
Guacamole, 35

Ham
    Broccoli-Ham Quiche, 162
    Calico Ham Slices, 142
    Ham and Egg Sandwich Cups, 14
    Ham 'n' Swiss on Rye, 182
    Hay and Straw, 170
Hot Crabmeat Sandwiches, 147
Hot Slaw, 125

Individual Cheesecakes, 67
Individual Meat Loaves, 98

Jam, Easy Strawberry, 28

Kiev, Chicken, 203

Lamb Patties, Minted, 192
Lasagna
    Florentine Lasagna Roll-Ups, 58
    Twosome Lasagna, 96
Lemon-Lite Green Beans, 101
Lemon-Sauced Kiwifruit and
    Strawberries, 206
Lemony Lite Pie, 225
Lemony Pear Delight, 212
Lemony Shrimp Fajitas, 34
Light and Lovely Cheesecake, 220
Lime Soufflé, Cool, 223
Lite Caesar Salad, 49
Lite Dessert Sauce, 85
Lite Maple Syrup, 28
Lite Spaghetti Parmesan, 51
Lite Yogurt Salad, 123
Lo-Cal Baked Potatoes, 119
Lo-Cal Strawberry Milk Shake, 77

Macaroni and Cheese, Colorful, 54
Main Dishes
    All-American Pizza, 44
    Colorful Macaroni and Cheese,
        54
    Florentine Lasagna Roll-Ups, 58
    Green Bean Moussaka, 40
    Hay and Straw, 170
    Make-Ahead Manicotti, 172
    Paella, 160
    Pork Lo Mein, 140
    Shrimp Primavera, 32
    Tuna-Vegetable Casserole, 134
    Turkey Club Casserole, 124
    Turkey-Pasta Toss, 122
    Twosome Lasagna, 96

Zucchini-Cheese Casserole, 144
Make-Ahead Manicotti, 172
Make-Ahead Meals, 149
Make-Ahead Oatmeal Muffins, 163
Mandarin Pork Medallions, 38
Manicotti, Make-Ahead, 172
Marinated Garden Salad, 45
Marinated Vegetable Medley, 173
Marinated Vegetables, 201
Meat. See also Beef, Ground Beef
    Individual Meat Loaves, 98
    Minted Lamb Patties, 192
Meatballs
    Beefy Meatball Minestrone, 42
    Freezer Meatballs, 177
    Meatball Stroganoff, 177
    Meatballs Bourguignon, 179
    Meatballs with Spaghetti Sauce,
        178
Mexican Egg Roll-Ups, 12
Mexican Rice, 35
Mexican Spoon Tacos, 186
Microwave Cooking Tips, 5
Milk Shake, Lo-Cal Strawberry, 77
Mini-Meals, 63
Mini Reuben Pitas, 84
Minted Lamb Patties, 192
Mocha Coffee, 27
Moo Goo Gai Pan, 52
Morning Frittata, 20
Moussaka, Green Bean, 40
Mousse, Very Berry, 210
Muffins
    Apple-Bran Muffins, 143
    Corn Bread Muffins, 43
    Make-Ahead Oatmeal Muffins,
        163
    Top-of-the-Morning Bran
        Muffins, 25

Noodles, Poppy Seed, 103

Oatmeal, Banana-Date, 11
Oatmeal Muffins, Make-Ahead, 163
Omelet
    Asparagus Omelet, 80
    Vegetarian Omelet, 74
One or Two, Meals for, 91
Onion Topper Tomatoes, 107
Oranges
    Ambrosia Oranges, 69
    Orange Chiffon Pie, 218
    Orange Sorbet, 228
    Oragne Whip, 11
    Spiced Orange Tea, 21

Oriental Fruit Compote, 141

Paella, 160
Pancakes
    Blueberry Shortstacks, 26
Parmesan Italian Bread, 157
Parmesan Oven Fries, 101
Pasta
    Colorful Macaroni and Cheese,
        54
    Fettuccini with Vegetables, 94
    Hay and Straw, 170
    Lite Spaghetti Parmesan, 51
    Poppy Seed Noodles, 103
    Pork Lo Mein, 140
    Shrimp Primavera, 32
    Spinach Spaghetti, 115
    Tortellini Salad, 66
    Turkey-Pasta Toss, 122
Pea Pods and Carrots, 169
Peaches
    Cheesy Peach Halves, 43
    Peach Melba, 208
    Peaches Flambé, 216
    Summertime Fruit Cup, 75
    Waffles with Peach Sauce, 18
Pears
    Lemony Pear Delight, 212
    Pear Crisp, 79
    Pears with Raspberry Sauce, 206
Peas, Dilled Fresh, 113
Peasant Chicken, 106
Pepper Steak, 188
Peppermint Fluff Pie, 224
Peppers, Colorful Stuffed, 164
Pies
    Lemony Lite Pie, 225
    Orange Chiffon Pie, 218
    Peppermint Fluff Pie, 224
Pilaf
    Quick Rice Pilaf, 117
    Rice Pilaf, 203
    Vegetable-Rice Pilaf, 47
Piña Colada Sherbet, 220
Pineapple-Orange Squares, 165
Pita Triangles, 161
Pizza
    All-American Pizza, 44
    French Bread Pizzas, 184
    Salad Pizzas, 88
Poppy Seed Bread, 59
Poppy Seed Noodles, 103
Pork
    Mandarin Pork Medallions, 38
    Pork Lo Mein, 140

Pork Tenderloin Patties, 138
Sweet and Sour Pork, 195
Potatoes
Buttered New Potatoes, 61
Chicken-Stuffed Potatoes, 128
Chunky Potato Salad, 167
Creamy Potato Puffs, 189
Dilly New Potatoes, 31
Freezer Twice-Baked Potatoes, 191
Lo-Cal Baked Potatoes, 119
Parmesan Oven Fries, 101
Potatoes au Gratin, 99
Taco Potato Wedges, 127
Whipped Potatoes, 153
Power Levels, 5
Primavera, Shrimp, 32
Pudding
Caramel Flan, 207
Chocolite Dessert, 214
Creamy Almond Custard, 207
Creamy Strawberry Tapioca, 213
Lemony Pear Delight, 212
Toasted Coconut Pudding, 210

Quiche, Broccoli-Ham, 162
Quick and Easy Meals, 121
Quick Creamy Beans, 97
Quick Fruit Cobbler, 211
Quick Garlic Rolls, 95
Quick Rice Pilaf, 117
Quick Spinach Salad, 139
Quick Veggie Soup, 148

Raspberries
Pears with Raspberry Sauce, 206
Very Berry Mousse, 210
Reuben Pitas, Mini, 84
Rice
Chicken and Rice Soup, 56
Chicken-Vegetable Rice Mold, 156
Fish with Creole Rice, 112
Fluffy Parsleyed Rice, 53
Fluffy White Rice, 197
Mexican Rice, 35
Paella, 160
Quick Rice Pilaf, 117
Rice for Two, 105
Rice Pilaf, 203
Vegetable-Rice Cups, 193
Vegetable-Rice Pilaf, 47
White and Wild Rice, 159
Rotating, Stirring, and Turning, 6

Salad Pizzas, 88
Salads
Ambrosia Oranges, 69
Asparagus and Beef Vinaigrette, 82
Bacon-Topped Tomato Slices, 135
Cheesy Peach Halves, 43
Chicken-Vegetable Rice Mold, 156
Ching Chang Salad, 68
Chunky Potato Salad, 167
Freezer Coleslaw, 183
Fresh Fruit Gelatin Salad, 55
Frozen Mini Fruit Salads, 185
Hot Slaw, 125
Lite Caesar Salad, 49
Lite Yogurt Salad, 123
Marinated Garden Salad, 45
Marinated Vegetable Medley, 173
Marinated Vegetables, 201
Pineapple Orange Squares, 165
Quick Spinach Salad, 139
Shrimp Salad in Tomato Cups, 70
Spinach Salad, 169
Spinach Salad Supreme, 57
Tarragon Chicken, 86
Tomato Aspic Salads, 151
Tortellini Salad, 66
Salmon Timbales with Cucumber Sauce, 136
Sandwiches
Bacon Cheeseburgers, 100
Bacon-Tomato Sandwiches, 148
Ham and Egg Sandwich Cups, 14
Ham 'n' Swiss on Rye, 182
Hot Crabmeat Sandwiches, 147
Lemony Shrimp Fajitas, 34
Mini Reuben Pitas, 84
Scrambled Muffinwiches, 180
Stuffed Pita Pockets, 200
Terrific Turkey Tostadas, 72
Veggie Rounds, 65
Sauces
Lemon-Sauced Kiwifruit and Strawberries, 206
Lite Dessert Sauce, 85
Peaches Flambé, 216
Pears with Raspberry Sauce, 206
Savory Chicken Rolls, 50
Savory Italian Green Beans, 133
Savory Squash, 99
Scallops
Scallops Supreme, 132

Seafood Supreme, 158
Scampi, Shrimp, 116
Scrambled Muffinwiches, 18
Seafood Supreme, 158
Sequence for Cooking Meals, 6
Sesame Broccoli and Carrots, 37
Sherbet, Piña Colada, 220
Sherried Carrots, 171
Shortstacks, Blueberry, 26
Shrimp
Lemony Shrimp Fajitas, 34
Seafood Supreme, 158
Shrimp Primavera, 32
Shrimp Salad in Tomato Cups, 70
Shrimp Scampi, 116
Skewered Beef Teriyaki, 168
Sliced Beef with Mustard Sauce, 166
Sliced Cinnamon Apples, 209
Snacks
Apple S'mores, 73
Apples and Cheese, 131
Banana-Orange Push-Ups, 223
Fruit-Nut Balls, 71
Granola Bars, 76
Sole Oscar, 30
Soufflé
Chocolate-Almond Soufflé, 208
Cool Lime Soufflé, 223
Creamy Strawberry Soufflé, 211
Fruit Cream, 217
Soup
Beefy Meatball Minestrone, 42
Chicken and Rice Soup, 56
Chili, 64
Creamy Zucchini Soup, 146
Egg Drop Soup, 108
Quick Veggie Soup, 148
Vegetable-Clam Chowder, 78
Wonton Soup, 194
Spaghetti Sauce, Meatballs with, 178
Spiced Orange Tea, 21
Spinach
Florentine Lasagna Roll-Ups, 58
Florentine Rolls, 152
Quick Spinach Salad, 139
Spianch Salad, 169
Spinach Salad Supreme, 57
Spinach Spaghetti, 115
Squash, Savory, 99
Steak Diane, 118
Strawberries

Berry Cream Squares, 219
Berry-Filled Angel Food, 215
Creamy Strawberry Soufflé, 211
Creamy Strawberry Tapioca, 213
Easy Strawberry Jam, 28
Frozen Strawberry Cream, 226
Fruit Cream, 217
Lemon-Sauced Kiwifruit and
    Strawberries, 206
Lo-Cal Strawberry Milk Shake,
    77
Summertime Fruit Cup, 75
Very Berry Mousse, 210
Stroganoff for Two, 102
Stroganoff, Meatball, 177
Stuffed Dilled Sole, 114
Stuffed Pita Pockets, 200
Sugar-Glazed Grapefruit, 24
Summertime Fruit Cup, 75
Sweet and Sour Pork, 195
Swiss Steak, 190
Syrup, Lite Maple, 28

Taco Potato Wedges, 127
Tacos, Mexican Spoon, 186
Tapioca, Creamy Strawberry, 213
Tarragon Carrots and Zucchini, 103
Tarragon Chicken, 86
Tea, Spiced Orange, 21
Teriyaki, Skewered Beef, 168
Terrific Turkey Tostadas, 72
Toasted Coconut Pudding, 210
Toasted Garlic Sticks, 145

Tomato Drink, Zippy, 13
Tomatoes
    Bacon-Tomato Sandwiches, 148
    Bacon-Topped Tomato Slices, 135
    Green Bean-Filled Tomatoes, 120
    Onion Topper Tomatoes, 107
    Shrimp Salad in Tomato Cups,
        70
    Tomato Aspic Salads, 151
Top-of-the-Morning Bran Muffins,
    25
Tortellini Salad, 66
Tostadas, Terrific Turkey, 72
Tuna-Vegetable Casserole, 134
Turkey
    Stuffed Pita Pockets, 200
    Terrific Turkey Tostadas, 72
    Turkey Club Casserole, 124
    Turkey Cordon Bleu, 154
    Turkey-Pasta Toss, 122
TV Dinner Tips, 202
Twosome Lasagna, 96

Vegetable-Rice Pilaf, 47
Vegetables. See also individual types
    Cheesy Vegetables, 129
    Chicken and Veggie Bundles, 104
    Chicken-Vegetable Rice Mold,
        156
    Fettuccini with Vegetables, 94
    Fresh Vegetable Platter, 155
    Marinated Garden Salad, 45
    Marinated Vegetable Medley, 173

Marinated Vegetables, 201
Quick Veggie Soup, 148
Salad Pizzas, 88
Savory Squash, 99
Tuna-Vegetable Casserole, 134
Vegetable-Clam Chowder, 78
Vegetable Medley, 111
Vegetable-Rice Cups, 193
Vegetarian Omelet, 74
Veggie Rounds, 65
Very Berry Mousse, 210

Waffles with Peach Sauce, 18
Waldorf Stuffing, Chicken with, 48
Whipped Potatoes, 153
White and Wild Rice, 159
Wonton Soup, 194

Yogurt
    Cherry-Almond-Topped Frozen
        Yogurt, 216
    Frozen Yogurt Cups, 228
    Lite Yogurt Salad, 123
    Yogurt and Granola, 83
    Yogurt-Fruit Bowl, 16

Zippy Tomato Drink, 13
Zucchini
    Creamy Zucchini Soup, 146
    Tarragon Carrots and Zucchini,
        103
    Zucchini-Cheese Casserole, 144